Explorations in Theology 6

Explorations in Theology 6

DON CUPITT

SCM PRESS LTD

334 01976 1

First published 1979
by SCM Press Ltd
58 Bloomsbury Street, London WC1

Photoset by Input Typesetting Ltd
and printed in Great Britain by
Billing & Sons Ltd
Guildford and Worcester

Contents

Introduction

It is unwise to trust people's accounts of the development of their own thinking too much, not only because memory is an inveterate liar but also because hindsight alters judgment. This collection, containing a number of essays that have not previously appeared in book form, opens with an early piece called *'What is the Gospel?'* When I wrote it in 1964 I was one of those serious hyper-orthodox young men who arise in each generation to dismay their elders and betters (just as today, replicas of what I was, they have arisen to reproach *me*). The essay seemed at that time to be a conventional protest against the Christian atheism then fashionable, and indeed was the first and last of my writings to receive the august *imprimatur* of Dr E. L. Mascall's approbation. But if it deserves reprinting now it is not for that reason, but because with hindsight one can also see in it a different argument, here being advanced for the first time, to the effect that the Christ-centred theology which had been popular for so very long was in fact on the brink of atheism. Paul van Buren (himself a former pupil of Karl Barth) only had to give it one nudge, and it toppled over. Christ-centred Christianity must eventually evolve into human-ism, and so lose touch with everything that Jesus himself had stood for.

The second essay is about a question in medical ethics. Not many theologians write about specific ethical problems nowadays, and this piece may seem something of an odd man out. But in 1969 heart transplants were new and were attracting the usual public response – anti-science populism and religious obscurantism overlaid with a good deal of huffing and puffing about 'serious ethical and moral questions'. I wanted to suggest that the moral questions are not insoluble, and there is no reason to be fearful. Twenty years ago the late George Woods said to me, 'It doesn't look like it now, but one day we may find we are having to defend the scientists.' There is some connexion between this piece and the protest against the revival of exorcism in no. 6. Among religious people there is often to be found a sentiment of fear and dislike of the natural sciences, and a wish to revert to a pre-scientific outlook. I believe this to be a temptation that must be resisted.

If one accepts the scientific outlook one must reject anthropomorphic and interventionist ideas of God. The world about us is continuous natural process, without any hidden wire-pulling. My own background is in natural science, empiricist (and more recently, post-Kantian) philosophy, and in the old long-secularized industrial England. Though temperamentally very religious, I have never looked for or believed in miracles, answers to prayer, particular providences or the 'supernatural' in the popular sense. Hostility to anthropomorphism was reinforced by my experience as a member, after my conversion, of a conservative and pietistic Protestant group. The curiously powerful psychological tyranny which that group exercised over its members depended upon an uncritically literal use of religious language. You had to say you 'knew the Lord', but you were not allowed to question precisely what could be *meant* by a claim to 'know' the Lord. Ever since, I have equated anthropomorphism with bondage to idols, and the negative way with spiritual freedom. The negative way, the only way to the true God, is by a sustained critique of religious imagery and a determined attempt to purge onself of religious illusions. Later, I was to be much influenced by Feuerbach, Freud and Durkheim, and to believe that Christian thought today must start from a candid recognition that much, perhaps most, of religion is indeed socially-induced human projection.

So in the late 1960s I spent a good deal of time studying the doctrine of analogy in English theology, being especially attracted to a line of tough-minded but now almost-forgotten theologians who included William King, Peter Browne, William Law, Edward Copleston and H. L. Mansel. The papers I wrote then are perhaps too dull and bookish to deserve reprinting here, but I have included the last of the series, one on Maurice which has not appeared in Britain before. I like Maurice as a bold theological revisionist, and his attempt to demythologize life after death points forward to no. 4 and to some of the later items in this book, but I could not help noticing how unashamedly much in Maurice's theology is a projection upon God of Maurice's own very Victorian ideals. God has got to be what Maurice feels God *ought* to be. There are more illustrations of the nineteenth-century 'moral projection' view of God in *Crisis of Moral Authority* (Lutterworth Press 1972), ch. 1.

The debate with Professor Moule is a genuine private correspondence between friends and colleagues, written at first without thought of publication. We later read it at a meeting and were urged to publish it, and I am grateful to Professor Moule for allowing me to reprint it because it aroused a good deal of comment when it first appeared. In courtesy I should refer the reader, for a more definitive statement of Professor Moule's views, to his Introduction to the 1968 symposium that he edited, *The Significance of the Message of the Resurrection for Faith in Jesus Christ* (SCM Press), and to his paper, 'The Christ of Experience and the Christ of History' (*Theology* LXXXI. 681, May 1978, pp. 164–72).

No. 5, on Darwinism, was originally written for the group which produced *Man and Nature* (ed. Hugh Montefiore, Collins 1975). It first hinted at unease with the traditional English science-and-religion synthesis, as it was restored by the liberal Catholic theologians of Charles Gore's generation.

The Open Letter on Exorcism was signed by sixty-five theologians and others, and originally issued to the Press on 15 May 1975. Professor G. W. H. Lampe and I drafted it and collected the signatures, but we know of nowhere where the text was published in full, so Professor Lampe has agreed with me that this is a convenient opportunity to put it on record. I have added a short note on the vigorous controversy that followed. Several passages in his book *God as Spirit* (OUP 1977, pp. 50–59, 110, 198–201) indicate why Professor Lampe felt so strongly about the issue. One benefit of the controversy, which we fought hard for many weeks, was (I like to imagine) that it helped forward the thinking that went into that fine book.

No. 7 was the last short piece in which I still, after a fashion, defended the traditional Trinity-and-Incarnation Christian cosmology. I linked the Father with cosmic order, the Son with the social and historical dimension of religion, and the Spirit with the concern for transcendence and individual spiritual freedom, Christian theism being a synthesis of the three concerns. I was writing *The Worlds of Science and Religion* (Sheldon Press 1976) and was still struggling after a Christian cosmology. But it was a swan-song, for another line of thought was about to supersede it.

Having already moved so much in my own views, I believed at the beginning of the 1970s that God could be known through the dynamic movement of the spiritual life, through the interplay of religious images and in particular by the way one image cancels another. The breaking of an idol is a pointer to the Transcendent. *Christ and the Hiddenness of God* (Lutterworth Press 1971) illustrates that point of view. Then in 1973, while writing *The Leap of Reason*, I tried to go beyond symbolism altogether in a dialectical movement of Spirit. God really is beyond all imagery, and therefore cannot be known through *any* cosmology or way of symbolically ordering the world of experience. God only appears when the ordered world passes away altogether, and can only be known in the darkness of an act of pure self-transcendence.

It was at this moment that I began to return to the historical Jesus and to see – very dimly at first – the point of his message. In fact *The Leap of Reason*, which was eventually published by Sheldon Press in 1976, was intended as a veiled interpretation of Jesus, but it was cast in a strongly philosophical style and nobody noticed its meaning. I have included a Radio 3 script of 1975, 'The Last Man', because, though very compressed, it makes some of the connections here.

Now the Incarnation is a basically world-affirming and cosmological doctrine, which hallows the present era, its affairs and concerns, and (all too often) the powers that rule it. But Jesus, I was increasingly seeing, owed his revelatory power to the fact that he was basically anti-cosmological and world-denying. As eschatological prophet he shows the true God because he stands spiritually at the end of the world, where everything but God has passed away. In that moment, when we face absolute annihilation, even the Incarnation has passed away and become irrelevant: there is nothing but God that can save us. So the more highly I came to revere Jesus the teacher, the more I was drawn away from the cosmology of Christendom and the doctrine of the Incarnation. From 1976 my allegiance belonged to the historical Jesus, and I began to regard the divine Christ of ecclesiastical faith as an historical and human product.

The first public indication of all this was a BBC–1 television script of June 1976. I reproduce the transmission script, though it is very faulty because such scripts are always the product of enforced last-minute compromises, revisions and patchings. During the same summer I was asked to write and present a long TV documentary to be called *Who was Jesus?*, and (in the same week) to join the group which was writing *The Myth of God Incarnate* (SCM Press 1977). I had some intimation of what the price would be for accepting these invitations but in the end I held my nose and jumped in, hoping that the troubles ahead would force me to clarify what I believed. 'Myth Understood', no. 10 in the present collection, shows the position I had reached by February 1978.

The last three items have to do with man and ethics. 'Man, Bound and Free', written in December 1976 or thereabouts, looks back to *The Leap of Reason* and forward to a recent small science-and-religion book called *The Nature of Man* (Sheldon Press 1979). No. 12, 'Critical Christian Ethics', was written in about May 1977 and attempts to relate the varying moralities of church history to Jesus' 'kingdom ethic', and to say something about philosophical ethics. Finally, in 'The Ethics of this World and the Ethics of the World to Come' (written December 1978) I have moved further to the left and towards a radical Protestant position. Christian morality is not to be seen as any sort of supplement to or validation of worldly and natural morality, but as a continual critique of it. The Christian's relation to the world, following Jesus, must be one of perpetual dissatisfaction with and rejection of the old order, combined with longing for and living by the power of the new order. The philosophy of spirit of 1973–5 has shifted somewhat. At that time (as in no. 8) I saw Jesus as a figure almost like the Buddha. Now I am trying to relate our experience of God to our ethical and historical existence. *Jesus and the Gospel of God* (Lutterworth Press 1979) attempts to take the decisive step forward from ecclesiastical faith to kingdom-faith.

It has been a hard road and I am not at the end of it yet, by any means. If I have told the story in some detail, it is not because I have a high opinion of the merits of the many things I have written this last dozen years. On the contrary, I have been very slow and clumsy, struggling with ideas much too big for me and doubtless often badly wrong. But a great many people seem to be untroubled in their own faith – or lack of faith, as the case may be – and they just do not understand why theologians make such heavy weather of what is to them essentially a simple business. It is rather uncommon for a theologian to attempt to explain what he has been up to. So I have tried, though I warned the reader at the beginning of the limitations of such an account as I have given. Those who intensely dislike my views can at least console themselves with the thought that they are still changing!

Six of these essays first appeared in the journal *Theology*:

1, 'What is the Gospel?' in vol. LVII, no. 530, August 1964, pp. 343ff.;

2, 'Transplanting the Heart', in vol. LXXII, no. 590, August 1969, pp. 341ff.;

4, 'The Resurrection: A Disagreement', in vol. LXXV, no. 628, October 1972, pp. 507ff.;

5, 'Darwinism and English Religious Thought', in vol. LXXVIII, no. 657, March 1975, pp. 125ff.;

10, 'Myth Understood', in vol. LXXXI, no. 684, November 1978, pp. 417ff.;

11, 'Man, Bound and Free', in vol. LXXX, no. 674, March 1977, pp. 100ff.

Three others appeared in other periodicals:

3, 'The Language of Eschatology: F. D. Maurice's Treatment of Heaven and Hell', in the *Anglican Theological Review* LIV, no. 4, Evanston, Illinois, October 1972, pp. 305ff.;

7, 'The Meaning of Belief in God', in the *Cambridge Review*, vol. 96, no. 2224, 31 January 1975, pp. 62f.;

12, 'Critical Christian Ethics' (under the title 'Whither Personal Ethics?'), in the *Modern Churchman*, vol. XXI, nos. 2–3, Summer 1978, pp. 72ff.

I am grateful to the Editors concerned for their kind permission to reprint them here.

Cambridge   D. C.
April 1979

1

What is the Gospel?

Is Christian faith ultimately about God or about Jesus? Is the gospel a message about God, namely that he is not only our Judge but, through Jesus, our Father? Or is it a message about Jesus, namely that this man of whom we tell is all of God that we can know or need to know? Many people will reply, 'Both, of course. God, the holy one whom we feared, is the Father of Jesus, and Jesus, the man like us, is the only Son of God. The gospel is a double statement, the good news of the union of God and man in Jesus.' But this unity has been sundered. There has long been a distinction between theocentric and Christocentric emphases in Christian doctrine; but it is now widening into a distinction between theistic and non-theistic interpretations of the gospel message. 'Christian atheism', as an alternative to traditional faith, is being discussed and must be examined. It is now a real question whether the gospel is basically about God or about Jesus.

Traditional Christianity sees the gospel as about *God*. In it prayer has been addressed to the Father, through the Son, in the Spirit. The anaphora of the Liturgy of Addai and Mari, in its original form, was addressed to Jesus only, and in this respect is so strikingly exceptional as to prove the rule in the only legitimate sense of that phrase. The historic mainstream of faith was and is undeniably theocentric, a *religion*. The gospel message is a message about God's disposition to us sinners. It asserts that God's disposition towards us is not as we feared. Rather it is holy love, justifying the ungodly, maintaining its own righteousness not in condemning us, but in vindicating us. The apostolic testimony to what God has done in Jesus Christ is offered as evidence for this gospel about God's forgiveness. The rational connexions between the testimony about Jesus and the good news about God are highly complex, and have as yet been only very partially unravelled. There has, for example, long been a dispute among theologians about whether God's disposition towards us may be said to have changed as a result of his work in Jesus; or whether it would be better to say that his true and unchangeable character is first disclosed in Jesus. But in either case, whether the cross of Jesus has opened a fresh way or signposted an old one, the root of the matter is the same. The gospel claims that God is more favourable to us than we had reason to hope, and offers in support of this claim the testimony about Jesus. The good news is about God: about God as Jesus shows him to be, about God as known in Jesus; but nevertheless, about *God*.

It is plain that on this account we have some knowledge of God before the gospel. It cannot be *merely* knowledge *that* he exists, because to know that something exists is not to know anything unless it is known *what* exists. The gospel states that it is the holy God in whom we already believed, whom ignorantly we worshipped, whose true nature is now finally declared in Jesus. It is not Jews alone who know enough of God to know of whom it is that a message about God tells. In his letter to the Romans, and in the book of the Acts of the Apostles, St Paul asserts that Gentiles also have this knowledge. And so, if we say that Jesus is from God, manifests God, or is God, we are making a synthetic assertion. 'God' has meaning apart from Jesus so that 'God is disclosed in Jesus' is not a tautology like 'Jesus is disclosed in Jesus'. Nor is it only a misleading way of saying 'Jesus discloses himself' or 'Jesus is morally ultimate, or divine'. 'God is disclosed in Jesus' is a synthetic assertion. It asserts a relationship between two terms whose meaning may to some extent be ascertained independently. To this relationship there are familiar analogies. For example, by a trick of speech or gesture I may recognize in John a likeness to his father Zebedee – but only if I have previously made Zebedee's acquaintance. The notion of recognition only has sense if 'John is like his father Zebedee' is a synthetic assertion. Of course the analogy does not hold in all points because if I am told that John is like his father, without having met his father, I can still understand what is being said about John because I have previous experience of fathers and sons and of their likeness. Whereas in the case of Jesus if we do not have any previous experience of God and of the possible likeness of men to him (including the idea of a likeness so perfect as to justify the use of the analogy of the likeness between a father and his son), then the assertion 'Jesus is like God' cannot have *any* sense for us. Even in the case of John and Zebedee, if I say 'John is like Zebedee, but we can have no independent knowledge of Zebedee', my hearer may assent, but he can hardly *agree*. 'Likeness to Zebedee' has no content for one who does not know what Zebedee is like. And the same is true *a fortiori* of 'likeness to God'. And so if someone holds that we have no knowledge of God apart from Jesus, and also holds that it is revealed that Jesus is like God, then nothing can tell either for or against this alleged revelation except the authority of the revealer. Since the revealer is said to be the very God to whom the proposition first introduces us we run here into a most awkward circularity. The word 'self-authenticating' has been used to surmount this difficulty, but the mere invention of a word is seldom sufficient of itself to solve a problem.

It appears therefore that there is a fundamental instability in the neo-orthodox theology which has held that God is disclosed in Jesus and nowhere else. When we perceive this instability we can go one of two ways. We may continue to say that Jesus is related to God synthetically, and revive the question of natural theology; or we may say that Jesus is related to God analytically – at least so far as our present knowledge can go. Let us explore this latter alternative.

The Christian who holds that the gospel is more a matter of history than metaphysics, of Jesus than 'religion', may argue as follows. To hold that Christianity is basically a message about God and how his favour has been won is to make of it merely one religion among many. Christianity is Jesus as the human norm. He is its sole foundation. Since each historical man is (perhaps necessarily) unique, and since no other religion is related to its founder as Christianity is to Jesus, then to start with him makes the uniqueness of the gospel clear. Since the gospel is about the sole sufficiency of Jesus for man's salvation, to start from a God known before him is to create an internal contradiction in the gospel message. To accept the full rigour of the gospel's assertion of Jesus' sole sufficiency is to see that we know nothing of God apart from him, and therefore to relate Jesus to God analytically. Jesus is all of God we can know or need to know. To have seen him *is* to have seen the Father (the 'is' expressing identity).

The position thus arrived at may be interpreted in either a strong or a weak sense. A *speculative Christian atheist* entirely renounces 'God,' life after death, etc. A *practical Christian atheist* may hold only that 'God' and life after death are negligible for us at present, *in via*.

The logic of *practical Christian atheism* may be explained in

terms of our earlier analogy. Even if we have never met
Zebedee it is still possible to accept somebody's assurance that
John is like him and wait for the time when we *do* meet him.
We have only to admit that such an assurance cannot give us
as yet any idea of what Zebedee is like apart from our idea of
what John is like. When we do meet Zebedee we will no doubt
recognize him if it is true that John is indeed a good likeness,
and we have studied him (that is, John) sufficiently closely.
And if we have modelled ourselves on John and imitated him,
then when Zebedee appears we shall ourselves be like
Zebedee. But *at present* we can for all practical purposes
disregard Zebedee altogether. John is all of him we can know
or need to know. Indeed we can ignore Zebedee for all
theoretical purposes because we have no justification for
making any assertion about him which goes in any way beyond
an assertion about John. All we can do is to talk of John. In this
way a Christian atheism is possible which is, strictly speaking,
agnostic about God without necessarily categorically denying
his existence. Jesus is God enough to us now, though there
may be more to come when sight replaces faith. This point
explains the stress on eschatological fulfilment on the part of
those who wish to distinguish Jesus from God but cannot
justify the distinction *now*.

The stronger position which may be taken holds that 'God'
has been a harmful and is now a meaningless notion. Christian
faith is better and purer for its abandonment. And so Christian
atheism proper can be reached – what I have called *speculative
Christian atheism*.

Now Christocentric faith is no new thing. The bases of
membership of many Protestant associations have mentioned
only 'Jesus Christ as God and Saviour'. But persons who have
accepted such formulas did not, I think, for a moment expect
the new development. One now often meets Christians who
hold that we need not, cannot, or must not speak of God any
longer. Jesus is all of God that we can know or need to know.
To many people this view seems highly attractive. In an age of
acute metaphysical agnosticism or scepticism we may despair
of the attempt to solve the problems raised by theism and by
traditional Christology. We may be tired of Christian theology's
perennial search for a metaphysic. We may welcome a vastly
simpler interpretation of Christianity, the transformation of
theology into anthropology to which Feuerbach looked forward.

There is a further important point. The earliest people to put
forward such ideas were influenced by Bultmann's scepticism

about the possibility of gaining any historical acquaintance with Jesus of Nazareth. Professor R. B. Braithwaite, in his Eddington Memorial Lecture of 1955, *An Empiricist's View of Religious Belief*, went so far as to propose a non-theistic interpretation of Christianity which was compatible with the view that Jesus never lived. This was startling, and the lecture has won great celebrity. But since then Bultmann's successors have revived interest in the question of the historical Jesus. A vivid portrait of Jesus is now drawn, which claims to be far better founded than the ninteenth-century lives. There is little doubt that this work, now becoming familiar in the English-speaking world, will give great encouragement to those who believe a non-theistic exegesis of the gospel to be both possible and desirable, in spite of the difficulty of Jesus' own belief in and prayer to God his Father.

I conclude therefore that our situation at present obliges us to ask, what is the gospel? Is it a message about God, namely that he is not our enemy but the Father of Jesus, or is it a message about Jesus, namely that he is all of God that we can know or need to know? My own belief is that the traditional theistic interpretation of the gospel is substantially correct, and I have shown that we must lay claim to some knowledge of God prior to the gospel in order to maintain it. Study of the earliest Christian preaching shows that this was realized from the beginning, by St Paul and succeeding apologists. They began their preaching to the Gentiles by appealing to such knowledge of God, however little or erroneous, as their hearers already possessed. The gospel, in short, must presuppose a natural theology. This is my conclusion upon the book by P. A. Van Buren, *The Secular Meeting of the Gospel* (SCM Press 1963), which has prompted these reflections.

2

Transplanting the Heart

One reason for the excitement about heart transplants is the
unerring way in which they pinpoint and revive ancient
stereotypes and forgotten fears. Something of the kind happens
in many professional relationships: with the dentist it is a
standing joke. With the medical man it runs deeper. He cannot
help touching upon our buried fears, and perhaps his own. So
he has developed defences. He uses an excruciating professional jargon, and he subjects himself to a particularly stringent
professional code. Even so, the jargon is criticized, for its
supposedly mechanistic assumptions, and because it is felt to
be a device for excluding the laity. And the code is criticized
because it is framed entirely within the profession in matters
where the patient has after all an interest. But both the jargon
and the code are needed.

So the relations between the medical man and his client are
delicate. Their delicacy is latent in the overtones of the
preferred word *patient*. The peculiarly intense stresses of the
profession are not always sympathetically understood, because
the prospective patient is too absorbed by his own anxieties.

The patient is indeed prone to fantasy. There have been two
main stereotypes projected upon the medical profession by
public opinion. The first is three centuries old. In the
seventeenth century the scientific revolution mechanized our
picture of the world from top to bottom, and in particular
human and animal bodies. And this caused a colossal upheaval,
for the human body is the physical object which stirs our
feelings more than any other, and is of most metaphysical
importance to us. It is the very way in which we are present in
the world. Our attitude to our bodiliness is crucial for politics,
ethics and religion. The materialism of Thomas Hobbes runs
easily from physick to physics, from perception to politics.

If in the seventeenth century there was a kind of dissociation
of sensibility as traditional ways of responding to the world

and the new science fell apart, then medical men bore the brunt of it. See, for example, Sir Thomas Browne's *Religio Medici*, or recall the tale of Sterne's corpse being recognized on a Cambridge dissecting table. The medical man almost had to be either materialistic or, like Browne, markedly dualistic in outlook. The dissection of cadavers, the secularization of the body, earned him the reputation of an infidel, a materialist, a man who laid impious hands on nature's secrets. The stereotype here runs from Faust through Burke and Hare and on to Frankenstein and Hammer Films. It is not forgotten yet.

In the nineteenth century something different appears. With the rapid rise in standing of his profession comes criticism of the medical man as the bogus priest of bourgeois civilization. An early and eloquent example is Kierkegaard:[1] 'In our time it is the physician who exercises the cure of souls', and he continues in a vein of fierce sarcasm against the cosy worldliness of the new priesthood. Something like this is familiar in *The Doctor's Dilemma*: 'Every profession is a conspiracy against the laity', and the complacent way in which people exclaim 'Doctor's orders!' The professional ethical code was intended to reassure the patient, but critics thought they could see in it mystification and moral arrogance.

I mention these stereotypes not because they are particularly illuminating in themselves but because they have become part of the inner history of the profession, and to this day they may cloud thinking about such matters as organ transplantation. And perhaps debate within the profession is influenced by them in the well-known differences of temperament between surgeons and physicians. The surgeon may be a seventeenth-century man yet, and the physician a nineteenth.

The subject of organ transplantation is still a matter of intense debate. The first successful kidney transplant took place in 1954, in Boston; and the first successful heart transplant in 1967, in Cape Town. Literature upon the special problems of transplants is recent: the well-known book by Glanville Williams, *The Sanctity of Life and the Criminal Law* (1958) makes little mention of them.

A decade ago interest focused upon the situation of those who, through the application of special techniques, inhabit a kind of 'twilight zone' where it can no longer be said clearly whether they are alive or dead. It had long been known that 'the moment of death' is a legal fiction. But in popular thought, and in some legal codes to this day, the criteria of death have remained the cessation of heartbeat and respiration. But it is

precisely these functions which can be prolonged in patients
who according to other criteria are indubitably dead – absence
of brain activity, dilation of the pupils (mydriasis), absence of
all reflexes.

Should heartbeat and breathing be prolonged in such a case
by such means? On 24 November 1957 the Pope said there was
no moral obligation to persist with extraordinary means of
maintaining 'life' where there was no real hope of recovery.
What is to count as death for medical purposes is for medical
science to determine, and presumably the same goes for
lawyers. Christian theology has no special competence in the
matter. And moral theologians invoke the principle of 'double
effect' to make it clear that 'switching off the machine' in such
a case is not properly speaking causing the death of the
patient.[2]

In 1965 the Church Assembly Board for Social Responsibility
published *Decisions about Life and Death*, also much concerned
with the twilight zone.

Attention however had already begun to move to transplants.
Since renal grafts began there has been legislation in many
countries. The English Human Tissue Act 1961, for example,
followed Australian and in turn influenced Canadian legislation
and further interest in the legal aspects has been shown since.[3]

The twilight zone was itself an important new fact for the
public to assimilate. But what about the transplantation of
organs from twilight zone patients? The medical men replied
that the relevant organs remained re-usable for some time after
the machine was switched off, so there need never be any
question of beginning surgery before the patient was as dead
as anyone could wish. But the public felt that such an operation
needs preparation. It was hardly to be supposed that a patient
would first begin to be looked upon as a 'potential cadaveric
donor' only after the death certificate had been written. It was
replied that the profession exists to save lives and it could have
no motive for being hasty with one life in order, at vast trouble
and expense, to take a chance of saving another. The
imputation was simply absurd.

Sometimes it is suggested that the special interest in heart
transplants is the product of lay ignorance and the emotional
overtones of the word 'heart'. Some popular reactions have
indeed been crude; the influence of the old stereotypes is all
too apparent. But the reply is also too crude. It betrays the
seventeenth-century dissociation of sensibility in its implied
distinction between objective facts and subjective feelings

which should never be allowed to influence practical judgment. It is perfectly conceivable that there should be research techniques and even therapeutic procedures which are effective but morally intolerable. The profession itself of course recognizes this.

In any case, it is clear that the transplantation of the heart, lungs, liver, etc., raises moral questions. But what are they?

There are various sorts of transplant: *autotransplants*, for example of skin, from another part of the same patient's body; *isotransplants* between identical twins, which of course are also not rejected; *homotransplants* between different members of the same species, where there *is* a rejection problem; and lastly *heterotransplants* between different species, where the rejection problem is particularly difficult. Again, the donor may be clearly living or clearly dead, so that the question of obtaining a valid consent is fairly straightforward; or he may at the time when consent is sought be in the twilight zone, so that it is not. And the organ donated may be as dispensable to the donor as a pint of blood, or as indispensable as the heart or liver.

Heart transplants are clearly in the most difficult category on all counts. But there are still more reasons for anxiety.

One which has been little publicized so far is the problem of determining who is psychologically strong enough to be able to bear living under chronic renal dialysis, or with a foreign heart. Some, perhaps many, possible beneficiaries are not. But some one in desperate need of a major transplant surgery is not in the best condition for psychological evaluation. The surgeon takes, cannot but take, a terrible risk.

The consent question is complicated by the legal uncertainties of property in corpses. In earlier times in England corpses fell within the jurisidiction of the ecclesiastical courts. The common law regarded a corpse as a *res nullius* and there was, and still is, no property in it. However, the Human Tissue Act 1961 includes the phrase 'person lawfully in possession of the body', which for our purposes probably means the Hospital Management Committee. As to what may be done with a corpse, there are three interests to be consulted: the known wishes of the decedent, the wishes of the surviving spouse or next-of-kin, and the coroner. But the whole question is not yet as clearly defined as could be wished.

Medical men themselves very reasonably dislike importuning people newly bereaved, particularly since the consequent publicity will aggravate their distress. So at the moment an opting-out scheme is being actively canvassed in official circles and before public opinion. Probably there will be certain carefully-defined exceptions – minors, the mentally ill, prisoners – but otherwise everyone will be presumed unless he has chosen otherwise to have consented to the use of his organs after death. The choice whether to opt out will of course have to be made in full knowledge of the issues in order to satisfy moralists and lawyers. And people ought to be aware in advance of what choice their spouse or next-of-kin has made.

It is hard to see any solid objection to such a scheme provided that transplant surgery becomes established and successful and economic. The real benefits of it in such a case are bound to outweigh any cavils, again provided that the public fully understands and accepts the conditions under which surgical removal of organs may take place and is assured that these conditions are invariably fulfilled.

There is here clearly a distinction between the morality of the interim period during which a new technique is being pioneered – and during which we should be prepared to tolerate a high failure rate, high costs, and so on – and the morality of the established period when organ transplantation has become a matter of routine.

Various things must happen if this second stage is to be reached. It is plain that the medical profession must take the public fully into its confidence. The answer to bad newspaper publicity is not no newspaper publicity but better newspaper publicity. It is not satisfactory that the professional ethical code should be framed and enforced purely intra-professionally. The public must fully understand the nature of the twilight zone, the way in which the intensive care team looking after the donor is related or unrelated to the surgical team looking after the recipient, and the criteria upon which decisions are made. It may well be that the limited function of the coroner under the Human Tissue Act 1961 should in some way be extended so that a legal man can participate in the evolution of the professional code and represent the lay interest. He could usefully take some responsibility off the doctors. It is probable – or at least, one may guess – that no court anywhere will convict a doctor for switching off the life-support machine except in a case of the most serious professional negligence. But that is no excuse for leaving doctors in a situation of chronic legal compromise because the public is too timid to face facts.

It would seem then that the arrival of heart transplant

surgery is a matter of practical moral difficulty rather than of theoretical moral difficulty. By a practical moral difficulty I mean a situation where in general we know what norms there are, we know what should be done, but where what we have to do is complicated and it will be tricky to get it all right without errors of tact or judgment. By a theoretical moral difficulty I mean a situation so new that we do not know what the norms are, and do not know how to handle it at all.

The moral principles in a heart transplant situation are not difficult to discern. If there is a real probability of benefit to the recipient, and the donor (*a*) is clearly irrecoverable, (*b*) is not known to have expressed objection beforehand, (*c*) is not excluded by the wishes of the next-of-kin, and (*d*) may supply the organ(s) required without prejudice to someone who may be called to account for his death, then there can be no real objection, and that is that. The practical problem is simply to set up regular procedures to ensure that the various conditions are met. And this is being done.

I believe that this disposes of the familiar technical giants/ moral pygmies argument. For people suggest, as a reason for caution, that our technical powers have greatly outrun our ability to use such powers rightly. This is a misunderstanding. The formation of a solid moral consensus takes a long time. It requires full information, good communications and a wide-ranging debate. Naturally it must follow rather than precede the acquisition of a new technical power. And only when a moral consensus has been reached is it useful to ask if some part of it should be expressed in civil law.

What of the fundamental criticism that the treatment of cadavers as if they were obsolete machines which may be cannibalized for spare parts is repugnant because it violates our sense of ourselves, or is in some way an affront to human dignity?

It is not easy for a Christian moralist to be clear about this. Humanists, while acknowledging the duty to respect the wishes of the deceased, would presumably be very critical of any suggestion of sacredness attaching to corpses. For them the needs of the living must obviously take precedence over the physical integrity of a corpse.[4] The Christian, however, recalls Antigone and Tobit, the resurrection of the body and the veneration of relics, and may be confused. He has a suspicion that there are moral principles which should govern the treatment of corpses, but finds it difficult to express and defend them rationally.

My suggestion is that the decent treatment of corpses is an elementary prayer for the dead. That is, it is an expression of human solidarity and affection, and an affirmation that human kinship is unbroken by death. The dead man lives, as all men do, unto God.

But I agree with the humanist that there is nothing indecent or profane whatever in the use of organs from cadavers in the practice of medicine. For the aims of that practice are also moral aims, of a piece with the aims of the decent treatment of corpses.

A theoretical difficulty of the utmost gravity occurs in connexion with the use of human experimental subjects in the furtherance of medical research. The case I have in mind is this: sometimes it is necessary to eliminate a variable by *not* informing the experimental subjects that they *are* experimental subjects. It may be that in testing a drug you may need to deceive some of the subjects in order to test for the 'placebo effect'.

Moralists might help here, by examining such phrases as 'the value of the individual' and 'the sanctity of life'. They cannot be legitimately used to argue that in every possible case the interest of the individual ranks higher than that of the community at large. We admire a man who risks his own life knowingly in the cause of medical research. But what of a person whose life is risked without his knowledge, in the course of research for the purposes of which it is essential that he should be in ignorance? Legal controls will eventually no doubt be needed here,[5] but I think Christian moralists should not be afraid to try to define cases where the social interest overrides the individual, and to say that medical research can be one such case. After all, they put up with conscription for war.

My conclusion is that although there are numerous important practical problems ahead there is no reason why the Christian moralist should regard cardiac transplants with particular anxiety. They may well in time come to be regarded with as much composure as blood transfusions are now.

3

The Language of Eschatology:
F. D. Maurice's Treatment of
Heaven and Hell

F. D. Maurice's eschatological teaching is as distinctive and individual as his teaching on any other subject. He may have abhorred systematic thought, but to every subject he took up he brought his own remarkable personality. The coherence of his writings is the consistency of the man himself: *that* degree of 'system' he could not help imposing. So to introduce his eschatological teaching I shall present a few passages, roughly in biographical order.

On or about 6 February, 1832 Maurice wrote to his father an account of his 'feeling' about 'what you call doctrinal or speculative views'. In this letter Maurice says that the men of the Bible regarded communion with God, intimate personal fellowship with him, as the supreme good. This God was utterly holy and loving; sin was abhorrent to him; and so the hope of fellowship with such a God implied that 'he had some way of removing their sinfulness and imparting his own character to them'. This basic insight gives Maurice his criterion of religious truth. 'Just as any system of divinity helps me to realise these feelings, just so far do I believe it true.' The full statement follows:

> If I can honestly say of any doctrines, these teach me how I may converse with the holy and invisible God as a real person . . . how I may overcome the difficulties to this intercourse which arise from his being unseen, from the evident impossibility of my forming a notion of him by my own understanding, and from the unlikeness and dissimilarity of our characters; if they show me how my character may be conformed to his, not how his may be brought down to mine; if they inspire me with a desire for this intercourse, a delight in it, and a conviction of its reality, just so far as I can,

after strict examination, say this of any doctrines, just so far have
I a test that they are the doctrines of the Bible, the true doctrines.[1]

This criterion of religious truth was not entirely novel. Early
in the eighteenth century Robert Jenkin, author of a popular
book called *The Reasonableness and Certainty of the Christian
Religion*, said that though the doctrine of the Trinity was
admittedly incomprehensible, it was a good thing to believe it,
because so to think of God kindles the religious affections and
diposes the soul to obedience of the gospel.[2] In *Alciphron, or the
Minute Philosopher* George Berkeley said the same: why should
a man not believe in the Trinity 'provided that this doctrine . . .
makes proper impressions on his mind, producing therein
love, hope, gratitude and obedience?'[3] Jenkin was confuting
Deists, who considered that believing mysteries did nobody
any good, and Berkeley was replying to the empiricist objection
that the terms used in stating the doctrine of the Trinity were
meaningless because they had no ideas of sense annexed to
them. He claimed that theological terms were religiously and
morally useful, much as certain physical concepts like 'force'
are operationally useful. But neither Berkeley nor Jenkin, of
course, used the criterion of adequacy to religious and moral
experience in as thoroughgoing a way as Maurice.

The next passage is from a pamphlet in the form of an open
'Letter to a non-resident Member of Convocation' (*sc.*, at
Oxford), who was in fact Samuel Wilberforce, entitled *The New
Statute and Mr Ward* (1845). Ward had, in the previous year,
scandalized the University by declaring in *The Ideal of a Christian
Church* that the Thirty-Nine Articles were absurd, and that his
own assent to them was of the least literal sort. In retaliation it
was proposed to enact a Statute which in effect could be used
to enforce the most stringent form of assent imaginable.
Maurice, though the author of *Subscription no Bondage*,
demurred, saying that he understood two at least of the
Articles in a sense quite possibly different from that intended
by the Reformers who compiled them. The important case is
Article Seven, which declares that the Old Testament is not
contrary to the New, because in it as in the New everlasting life
(*aeterna vita*) is offered to mankind through Christ. Now, says
Maurice, the Reformers may quite possibly have meant a future
state by 'everlasting life'. But if so, then the Article ought not
be believed in its original sense, for two reasons: first, because
it is doubtful whether the men of the Old Testament did
believe in a future life; and, secondly, because 'nothing seems

to be so important for the interpretation of Scripture and the establishment of a sound theology as that the revelation of God, and not the notion of rewards and punishments, should be *felt* to be the end of the Divine dispensation.' And Maurice says he *does* believe the Article in the sense of the Fourth Gospel: 'This is life eternal, that they may know thee, the only true God, and Jesus Christ.'[4]

This passage is important for the interpretation of Maurice's eschatology. Running through much of Maurice's writing is a sharp hostility to the 'Old Bailey theology' which pictured God as dispenser of rewards and punishments after death. I suppose most people nowadays think of the sermon in Joyce's *Portrait of the Artist as a Young Man* as the great example of hell-fire preaching, but the real thing was much more extreme than that. Here, as a sample, is a passage from Jonathan Edwards' sermon 'Sinners in the Hands of an Angry God', preached at Enfield, New England, in 1741:

> The God that holds you over the pit of hell, much as one holds a spider, or some loathsome insect, over the fire, abhors you, and is dreadfully provoked: his wrath towards you burns like fire; he is of purer eyes than to bear to have you in his sight; you are ten thousand times more abominable in his eyes, than the most hateful venomous serpent is in ours. You have offended him infinitely more than ever a stubborn rebel did his prince: and yet, it is nothing but his hand that holds you from falling into the fire every moment.[5]

Like Maurice, Edwards is a preacher. It is not his purpose to write a guide-book to hell for the information of future residents, but to convert sinners. For Edwards, as much as for Maurice, the primary use of the language of eschatology is not descriptive, but hortatory. He wants to rescue sinners from the doom that threatens them. But the way he speaks implies a picture of God which does *not* pass Maurice's test. In the *Theological Essays* and elsewhere Maurice makes no bones about the horrific and repulsive picture of God implicit in such language, and the way in which it makes the love of goodness a matter of the lowest expediency.

But, and here is the crux, are we to understand Maurice as cutting out all reference to the future from his eschatological doctrine? It sometimes seems so. At the end of *The Kingdom of Christ* (1838), in the last paragraph of the note on the Athanasian Creed, Maurice is already to be found identifying eternal life with the knowledge of God, and hell with 'Atheism, the state of the human spirit left without God'. In *The New*

Statute and Mr Ward (1845) Maurice appears to be saying that the men of the Old Testament might well have understood the gospel of eternal life without believing in a future life. And in another note on the Athanasian Creed, printed at the end of the second (1854) and later editions of the *Theological Essays*, Maurice expressly repudiates what we might call 'inaugurated eschatology'. He says that he is using the word 'eternal' in a sense even 'peasants and women' understand. There is an eternal world about us, in which we live by prayers:

> There is an Eternal Life which is emphatically a present life (not according to a doctrine which I have listened to lately with astonishment, alike for its logic and theology – a *future* life begun in the present); and . . . this Eternal Life consists in the knowledge of God; and . . . the loss of knowledge of God is the loss of it.[6]

On the other hand Maurice does sometimes speak of the 'future' enjoyment of eternal life. The volume called *Christmas Day* (1843) contains his typical doctrine of eternal life and death, but it also contains, in the Easter sermon on 'The Resurrection of the Body', a strong statement of the Christian hope for life after death. What then is the relation between the gospel of present eternal life and the Christian's hope in the face of death? Perhaps the clearest passage is Note D at the end of *The Word 'Eternal' and the Punishment of the Wicked* (1853):

> It may seem to some that I have passed over the words in I John 2.25 – 'And this is the *promise* which he has promised us, even eternal life' – because I thought that they clashed with the other words which I have quoted [i.e., other passages in the same epistle]. Not at all; for, first, it is not said that the promise has not been performed; and secondly, I never doubted that eternal life is the blessing which we are to desire in a future world; which we are to hope for there in its fulness. The prayer of St Chrysostom . . . asks that we may have in this world knowledge of God's truth, and in the world to come that 'eternal life' which standeth in this knowledge. The hope is perfectly consistent with the gift; one would be impossible without the other. But if eternal life is *identified* with future life its meaning disappears, and we have a vague dream of felicity in exchange for the substantial blessings which God holds out to us.[7]

Maurice's position, so far as we have proceeded in our exposition of it, seems to be this: the term 'eternal' has nothing to do with duration. It is an attribute of God. Eternal life is God's mode of life, which he communicates to those whom he brings into fellowship with himself. Maurice deprecates any attempt to *define* eternal life; it should be felt, lived, and preached. But if a definition were to be attempted, it should contain no reference to the future, or indeed any other tense, except the biblical *Now*. Any such reference would be thoroughly misleading. An adequate phenomenological description of the state of eternal life enjoyed by believers, however, would include a reference to their hope of the future consummation of this state in another world.

Whether Maurice is entirely consistent here is hard to say. The phrase 'one would be impossible without the other' implies the assertion that the present gift of eternal life would be impossible without the hope of its future consummation in another world; which in turn seems to imply that the Christian experience of eternal life contains analytically an expectation that we shall have further experiences after our deaths.

It is a matter of great philosophical interest today whether a religiously adequate eschatology can be stated without any commitment to that belief. Let us be clear: Maurice himself did in some sense believe that we shall have further experiences after our deaths. The crux for the interpretation of Maurice is *whether he could have dispensed with* that belief. Is Maurice's gospel of eternal life as a present possession *logically* independent of claims about life after death?

On the one hand we might read Maurice as saying this: eternity has nothing to do with duration. My present enjoyment of eternal life is a gospel which frees me from the nightmare of an endless prolongation of my life after death. In the essay 'On the Resurrection' in the *Theological Essays* (1853), Maurice seems to run close to agreeing with Strauss that 'the last enemy which shall be destroyed is the belief of man in his own immortality'. So that I shall have further experiences after my death is not the basic *claim of* Christian eschatological preaching, but rather a kind of *dread from which* the gospel of eternal life will deliver us. As I enter now into fellowship with the eternal God the bogey-world of Sheol, Hades, the Underworld, Gehenna all drops aways. It ceases to terrify. I am in hands which I cannot fall out of, because I have passed beyond change: I am with the Eternal One.

On the other hand, Maurice very rashly insisted (because of his concern to deny the endlessness and futurity of hell-punishments) that the word eternal bears the same meaning in the two phrases, 'eternal life' and 'eternal death'. Obviously it does not, any more than 'perfectly' bears the same meaning in the two phrases 'perfectly beautiful' and 'perfectly hideous'. Eternal death is not a mode of God's being in which men may participate, in the way that eternal life is. But, given Maurice's own insistence on the symmetry of the two phrases, we may ask: Are they then *both* terminable states? On conversion a man passes from a state of eternal death to one of eternal life, as Maurice says. Can he pass the other way? Surely 'eternal life' has always been portrayed in symbols of indestructibility; ever-flowing fountains, unfading wreaths, gold and precious stones. Is it not a part of the notion of eternal life that when I enter this state I am conscious of being *secure* in it? And does not that security imply a future hope?

So on the other hand we may read Maurice as recognizing that though eternal life as such contains no reference to tense, yet, precisely because it is beyond the realm of change, change cannot threaten it. What is new in Maurice can be set out by contrasting him with Paley and Whately.

For Paley (and I caricature here quite deliberately) the Christian dispensation really begins to be put into effect at the Last Judgment. The expectation of that future event, which revelation tells us of, reaches back into the present life and gives us an incentive to right conduct. This life becomes Christianized, or coloured with religious significance, solely by virtue of the expectation of future judgment. Revelation is reduced to a system of rewards and punishments which, we have good reason to apprehend, will be put into effect after our deaths. It is rather as if universities make themselves educationally effective only in so far as fear of the examinations at the end of the year incites the students to work. How by such method can a disinterested love of learning be inculcated? My caricature of the 'Old Bailey theology' is roughly that which Maurice learned from Coleridge, and it was fiercely resented by Maurice's critics.[8] In this preaching, says Maurice, 'God is represented as the destroyer'; the disciples of Christ are taught 'to be afraid lest he who numbers the hairs of their head should be plotting their ruin'.[9] For the 'Old Bailey theology', the natural immortality of the soul and even the expectation of judgment were usually represented as matters of reason known to all men. The Christian revelation had been given to bestow upon men more exact information about the nature of the Last Judgment, the criteria by which it would be conducted, and the way by which men could obtain a sure hope of acquittal. This information was 'saving truth'.

Richard Whately, on the other hand, denied that the belief in a blessed immortality was general to mankind, and could be attained by natural reason. Life and immortality were brought to light by the gospel alone. Whately at least began to change the order of exposition: he started from the gospel and then went on to the hope of a blessed immortality which it brought.[10]

Maurice, though, thought that the fear of death and what might lie beyond it *were* universal to men. The Old Bailey theology openly reinforced these primeval fears. It built on them. But Maurice goes along with Whately in putting the gospel of God's love first, and then finds that it banishes fear. The fundamental axiom is the message that God is a holy and loving Father, who calls men into an eternal communion with himself. This exalts them to a region where death has lost its sting, and fears of what may lie beyond it can no longer make them afraid.

Now let us put to Maurice our modern question: 'Do you or do you not, Mr Maurice, expect further experiences after your death?' If we could give Maurice a modern voice in which to reply I think he would probably say that the question is ill-framed. This is *not* to answer the question in the negative. Perhaps I can put into Maurice's mouth a clearer reply: The supposition that the eternal God may let me fall out of his hands into nothingness at the moment of my death is inconsistent with what I already know of him; and indeed has no meaning, for it attributes temporal predicates to God. In my baptism I have already gone through the Last Judgment, I have already passed from death to life. In so far as I have entered into communion with the eternal God I have entered a state which death cannot change, because nothing can change it. From my end of the relationship, in so far as I still live and change in time, I can and must long to enter ever more deeply into the state of eternal life: but in so far as it is indeed the eternal God with whom I have to do I am anchored immovably.

Well, we have many more questions to ask about all this, but let us complete our exposition of Maurice himself. On 16 November 1849 the young F. J. A. Hort wrote a long letter to Maurice asking his help in the moral difficulties he felt over the doctrine of eternal punishment.[11] Maurice wrote, on 23 November, a long and careful reply which Hort copied and circulated among his friends: 'I was brought up in the belief of universal restitution; I was taught that the idea of eternal punishment could not consist with the goodness and mercy of God.'[12]

But, Maurice continues, the Unitarian God seemed altogether too good-natured and easy-going. Since everyone knew about

Maurice's Unitarian background, he was eager to protest that it was not the source of his ideas. In fact, however, Maurice, like Coleridge, undoubtedly felt the force of the old free-thinking and Unitarian moral criticisms of Christianity, and felt that 'orthodoxy' must be revised to meet them. Paley, too, had felt acutely the moral objections to hell. Even as an undergraduate he proposed the thesis, *aeternitas poenarum contradicit Divinis attributis* (the eternity of hell-punishments is contradictory to the divine attributes).[13] Watson, the famous Bishop of Llandaff, tells the story in his autobiography, referring back to Tillotson. Paley's solution in practice was to stress that the language of hell is figurative and should be taken in an admonitory sense.[14] But this escape will not suit Maurice. To make the deterrent effective it must be credible; you must insist that there actually is such a place. And if it does deter, and its use is God's method of inciting people to do good, you will feel obliged to heat up your language to Jonathan Edwards' temperature. And by then it is plain that a God who works upon men in such a way cannot be the God of Maurice's theology.

To return to Maurice's letter, he declares his faith that God has redeemed mankind-as-a-whole through Christ, and chosen the church to be the witness of that redemption. 'The *starting-point* of the Gospel, as I read it, is the absolute Love of God: the *reward* of the Gospel is the knowledge of that love.'[15] Eternal life is the knowledge of God, damnation is privation of God. All thought of time, all speculation about the intermediate state, about purgatory, even about an eventual general restitution, is irrelevant and indeed a symptom of a flight from the true idea of eternal life, which is so 'grand and awful', which 'belongs to our own inmost selves':

> My duty then I feel is this: 1. To assert that which I know, that which God has revealed, his absolute universal love in all possible ways, and without any limitation. 2. To tell myself and all men, that to know this love and to be moulded by it is *the* blessing which we are to seek. 3. To say that this is eternal life. 4. To say that the want of it is death. 5. To say that if they believe in the Son of God they have eternal life. 6. To say that if they have not the Son of God, they have not life. 7. *Not* to say who has the Son of God, because I do not know. 8. *Not* to say how long anyone may remain in eternal death, because I do not know. 9. *Not* to say that all will necessarily be raised out of eternal death, because I do not know. 10. *Not* to judge any before the time, or to judge other men at all, because Christ has said, 'Judge not that ye be not judged'. 11. *Not* to play with Scripture by quoting passages which have not the

slightest connexion with the subject, such as 'Where the tree falleth it shall lie.' 12. *Not* to invent a scheme of purgatory and so take upon myself the office of the Divine Judge. 13. *Not* to deny God a right of using punishments at any time or anywhere for the reformation of his creatures. 14. *Not* to contradict Christ's words, 'These shall be beaten with few, these with many stripes,' for the sake of maintaining a theory of the equality of sins. 15. *Not* to think any punishment of God's so great as his saying, 'Let them alone.'[16]

There are nine self-denying ordinances in these fifteen rules: evidently Maurice thought that the central gospel of eternal life was strong enough to make a good deal of agnosticism about details perfectly tolerable. The vital thing was to educate people, 'out of the carnal into the Christian idea of eternity'.

We could pursue the details of Maurice's thoughts on these matters a great deal further, for example by delving into his controversy with Mansel, by studying *The Epistles of St John* (1857) and the Preface to the second edition of *Patriarchs and Lawgivers* (1885), and so on. We might even, if we were gluttons for punishment, search Coleridge for the sources of Maurice's ideas, but it has been done already. For the moment we have enough to go one, provided we remember Pfleiderer's remark that Maurice's theology is 'more complicated than that of any other theologian'.[17]

It is clear that one thing Maurice is doing is to criticize over-literal and crude ideas of life after death. He is trying to revise eschatology to make it more consistent with what he takes to be the basic Christian insights into the nature of God and his relations with man. In Maurice's support it is possible to adduce a number of theological considerations, and I must sketch them at this point.

It is true that the Old Testament is by and large not particularly interested in the future life. It knows, of course, of the usual Bronze Age belief in an underworld of departed spirits, Sheol; but Sheol has nothing to do with God, and the people of God are forbidden to traffic with it. Sometimes eschatological beliefs begin to emerge, but they are based not on any diagram of the after-life, but on moral experience and the nature of God. Moralists make a contrast between a way that leads to life and a way that leads to death. (Deut. 30. 15–20; Jer. 21.8; Prov. 12.28 etc; Matt. 7.13f.). In time of persecution, when the afflicted righteous may be tempted to doubt the power and goodness of God, the idea of resurrection may appear; but its main purpose is not to map the future world, but rather to reassure believers about the character of God (Dan. 12.2f.).

Furthermore, the Christian tradition has continued many of these themes. The New Testament does not appear to teach that the souls of the blessed are transferred to another world, there to live on after their deaths. Indeed the bizarre symbolism of the early Christian apocalyptic envisaged the imminent destruction not only of this earth, but of heaven and hell as well, and the replacement of that entire 'three-decker' scheme of things with something new. There has been in Christian thought a long tradition of reaction against excessive otherworldliness, and the practices (indulgences, invocation of saints, multiplication of requiem masses) to which it readily gives rise. Christians have usually expressed disapproval of spiritualism, and have disdained any interest in psychical research on the ground that mere survival (for a time) is of no particular religious interest, and that it is a religious misdirection, like idolatry, to be preoccupied with personal survival to a degree which takes precedence over the love of God. Any Christian eschatology must be primarily about God and the triumph of his love, not primarily about securing our own immortality.

Furthermore, there is a strong New Testament and liturgical tradition of realized eschatology. In the first Christian sermon (Acts 2), eschatological statements are interwoven with the demand for repentance and baptism as they always have been in Christian preaching and liturgy. The baptized already live the life, taste the food, enjoy the blessings, and wield the powers of the Coming Age. They have died and risen with Christ.

Thus the first thing to be said about Maurice's doctrines is that they find a great deal of support in the historic Christian tradition.

Maurice's use of the word 'eternal' is a more difficult matter. Etymology is not on his side. *Aeternus* is derived through *aeviternus* from *aevum*, and matches quite closely such English words as 'ages', 'always' and 'ever'. The Greek *aiōnios* derives from the root *aei*, 'always'.[18] Thus the basic sense in both Greek and Latin is of an everlasting existence, and the same thought can be seen in Hebrew talk of God – for example in Psalm 90. It is convenient to use the term 'sempiternal' of that which endures for ever in this sense. The absolutely sempiternal is always real, at all times. The retrospectively sempiternal is everlasting in past time but may come to an end in the future, like the universe in Fred Hoyle's cosmology. The prospectively sempiternal came into being at a moment in time, but is thenceforth everlasting, like a human soul in Aquinas' theology.

But when Maurice uses the word 'eternal' he clearly means it to refer to that which is not conditioned by time in any way. He blames Locke for having analysed the eternal as being no more than the sempiternal.[19] Maurice's use of the word 'eternal' has an ancestry which can be traced and often has been traced through Parmenides, Plato, Augustine, Boethius and Aquinas. The claim is that God is timeless, and this timelessness is associated with other attributes of God: his immutability, impassibility, incorruptibility, immortality and so on. It is claimed that if we understand God as timeless we shall be able to glimpse the solutions of old puzzles about divine predestination and foreknowledge, and so on. On the other hand many recent writers have criticized the idea that God is timeless on the grounds that it has no clear meaning, that it does not in fact contribute much to the solution of the puzzles about the relation of God to the world, and that it is inconsistent with other things people want to say about God, such as that he is personal, that he responds to human need, that he is loving and active and so on.[20]

Maurice goes still further, not only calling God eternal, but saying also, and making it a foundation-stone of his teaching, that men still living in time can 'simultaneously' be participants in the divine eternity. He does not seem to be very vividly aware of metaphysical difficulties in so speaking. One can say of Schleiermacher and of Kierkegaard that for them the phrase 'eternal person' has within it at least some internal tension. In Kierkegaard, that God is an eternal person, who cannot change, gives a tragic flavour to our relations with him. In Maurice however, no tension results from calling God at once eternal and personal. In Kierkegaard eternity is in a way *opposed* to time. At least the concepts belong together, by opposition. But in Maurice the absence of these stresses suggests that something very odd has happened. Eternity has no relation to time as we usually understand it, not even one of opposition. Suppose where Maurice uses the word 'eternal' one were to substitute the word 'perfect'. Would there be any appreciable difference in the force of what he says?

I think Mansel, with his usual acuity, correctly grasped the point here. Mansel uses terms like 'time, 'self', 'truth', 'knowledge', and so on, in an exact and philosophical sense, but he finds he cannot argue with Maurice because Maurice uses all these words in a moral sense. 'I am not fond', says Mansel icily, 'of judging of doctrines by their supposed moral effect on the conduct of those who hold them' or, for that matter, of regarding a doctrine as 'the result of a certain state of temper and feeling' in the man who enunciates it. Mansel thought that you could not argue about the philosophy of perception with a man who shouted that we had a moral duty to hold a realist theory, and that to affirm as much settled the argument. For Maurice *time* is that which is passing away, which still clings to us, but from which we must rise; *self* is egoism from which we must escape; *truth* is an object of moral aspiration. Mansel felt defeated by a man who would merely preach at him, who saw all philosophical questions as issues in which we have a *moral* duty to take one side or the other.[21]

Thus we miss the point of Maurice's talk about eternal life if we find philosophical difficulties in it. Maurice is above all else a moralist and a man of feeling. He talks constantly about how he feels, and what he finds it his *duty* to believe. Maurice's theology is, after all, 'Germano-Coleridgean'.

So now we have arrived at something like this (and it is not my fault if expounding Maurice is like getting lost in a maze): Maurice's claim is that we can enter into a mode of being, a *moral* condition, of which we can say, this is absolute, death is merely relative. I no longer have reason to be troubled by what the passage of time may bring, or of what death and what may lie beyond it may bring. Maurice is a Platonist: what is supremely good is supremely real and enduring, and that is that.

We may conclude by relating Maurice to D. Z. Phillips, author of a recent book on *Death and Immortality* (1970). Phillips says that most recent English-speaking philosophers of religion have thought that to believe in immortality is to believe that we shall have further experiences after our deaths. Some, like A. G. N. Flew, argue that this latter supposition is clearly meaningless. The notions of death, of personal identity and activity, and so on are quite clearly such that there is no sense in the phrase 'life after death'. Others, like Peter Geach, think that we might, in some intelligible sense, conceivably go on living after our deaths. Phillips clearly thinks that Flew has the better of the argument, but what he really wants to question is the underlying assumption. Does an eschatology like the Christian really make the claim that we shall have further experiences after our deaths? The Oxford Aristotelians (to invent a label for them) seem to think that religious belief is only of philosophical interest in so far as it seems to make extraordinary quasi-empirical claims about such things as the existence of God, his actions in the world, the resurrection of Christ, and life after death. The business of the philosophy of religion is to isolate these claims, define their meaning, and (usually) demolish the arguments in support of them. Once that is done, religion is of no further philosophical interest. But this whole endeavour, Phillips thinks, is misconceived, because it rests upon a misunderstanding of the purpose of religious language and the role of religious ideas in our lives.

Like Maurice, Phillips strongly repudiates the idea that the function of an eschatology is to make morality rational, by showing that it will ultimately be to our advantage to be good. The idea of eternal life is the idea of a dying life in which I have renounced all consideration of my own self-interest and my own survival. An eschatology focused on life after death simply reinforces self-concern; and in fact, if we look closely at the idioms in which we speak of the soul, we see that it is not an immortal thing in us. Rather, to speak of the soul is to speak of my relation to God and to goodness. Eternal life, a life of self-renunciation in which I am given over to love, is the believer's supreme moral concept in terms of which he assesses his life now.[22]

Phillips does not mention Maurice. The debts he acknowledges in his writings are to Wittgenstein, Kierkegaard, Tolstoy, and Simone Weil. His description of the present meaning of eternal life is theologically much less rich than Maurice's. But he goes beyond Maurice in being willing to employ both philosophical and religious arguments against any notion of life after death. The admonitory function of talk about the last things becomes the whole meaning of such talk.

Maurice's arguments for shifting the *primary* reference of eschatological language to present experience are, I think, of some real weight. A futurist eschatology has all too often led to a degradation of morality, an unpleasant picture of God, and the substitution of dreams of future bliss for a religiously rich and active life here and now. Maurice was right, I think, in saying that you get a morally and religiously stronger construction if you begin from present experience and see the future hope as growing out of it, that if you begin from the four last things and then see consideration of them as influencing your present way of life. Maurice's treatment of eschatology is a good example of his chief merit as theologian:

an intimate union of moral passion with a talent for reordering old materials into new patterns. But I think he was wise not to go so far as Phillips in cutting out life after death altogether. St Paul says that not even death can separate us from the love of Christ. Phillips' analysis of this statement is too parsimonious to be religiously adequate. Maurice keeps more of its substance.

4

The Resurrection: A Disagreement
(A Correspondence with C. F. D. Moule)

For many years CFDM has lectured at Cambridge on the Theology and Ethics of the New Testament, beginning from the Easter belief. In the summer of 1971 he read the chapters on the resurrection in DC's *Christ and the Hiddenness of God*. There DC distinguished three main groups of theories about the meaning and grounds of resurrection belief: 'Event theories', 'psi- or vision theories', and 'theological theories'; attempting to eliminate the first two as incoherent, and to establish a form of the third. To believe in the resurrection, he maintained, is to make a theological interpretation of Jesus' life and death. In a letter CFDM challenged this opinion, and so began the following correspondence, here presented in an abridged and slightly revised form.

CFDM to DC, 31 August 1971

I have been wont to say, in a rough and ready way, that the broad choice is between the Bultmannian-type of theory (your 'Theological' theory), which treats 'resurrection' as the New Testament way of describing the salvific character of the death, and the Barthian-type, which claims that some act of God *revealed* the salvific character of the death. I have said that I am deeply attracted by the Bultmannian type, relieving one, as it does, of having to struggle with 'what happened', and offering a deep and satisfying doctrine of the death of Christ; but that, as it seems to me, it unjustifiably evades the awkward question: what *led* the disciples to so profound an insight into the death? Bultmann expressly admits that he doesn't know: only, the death was always preached *with* the resurrection. But that seems to me historically irresponsible. There must be some explanation of the genesis of this belief, and it is surely up to us to attempt to find it.

Now you maintain that, short of a crassly materialistic and literalistic 'Event'-type account (which you show to be unacceptable), the only alternative is either the 'Theological'-

type or the 'psi'-type; and your account of the latter makes it, also untenable.

But I have, for some years, found myself trying to formulate something which, though it may fall roughly into your 'psi' category, does not seem to me so easily dismissed; and I want to ask you for your reactions. What if the claim is that there is historical evidence for something, *viz.* the coming into existence of the Easter-belief, to account for which nothing within the scope of historical evidence appears to be sufficient?

In *form* this is, no doubt, exactly like arguing that so many people claim that they have seen a ghost that, although by definition it is something that can't be traced by physical tests, we've got to believe in its reality. But I submit that, in *content*, the Easter belief is something very much harder to refute in the way one might refute that sort of argument. Thus:

(a) There is a large number of people all sharing the same conviction, and there is the tenacity of the conviction, and its organic connexion with their whole outlook and way of life, as these subsequently emerge. (This is certainly not cogent by itself, but, cumulatively, I find it significant.)

(b) There is the non-derivability of the belief from the Old Testament or from Pharisaism. With respect, I don't for a moment think anything in the Old Testament could have *generated* it. Of course, when they had to hunt for proof-texts, they did their best; but I can think of nothing that would naturally lead in the direction of the distinctive Easter belief. The same with Pharisaic beliefs. These were assorted, and ran from the crudest literalism to the rather beautiful spirituality of Baruch; but I have been able to discover none which suggests the entry upon *eternal* life by an *individual*, *before* the wind-up of history: and it's *this* that one has to account for. Clearly the New Testament shows no reflection of any belief that Jesus had been *revived* back to the old mortal life; the (various) endings of the story, in the different gospels and the Acts, all indicate (in their different ways) that it was believed to be the absolute life of the new age; and yet, entered upon by an *individual*, ahead of time, instead of by *all* the righteous, out *beyond* history. I can see nothing that would naturally lead to this, in any antecedent set of beliefs.

(c) And this conviction, by itself, seems to have persisted and to have differentiated Christians from other Jews, till, unwillingly, they were squeezed out of the Synagogue. In most (or all?) other great movements, if one deems the main tenet mistaken, one can see some accompanying advantage or attraction to account for the survival of the movement. Here, I can find none.

It is this kind of consideration that still inclines me to say: Here are historically well-attested beliefs, to account for which I have to invoke something beyond history, something transcendent. The New Testament calls it the resurrection of Jesus; I don't pretend to know what that is, nor would I press the term; but I submit that it makes better sense to say that the Easter belief was generated by Jesus' aliveness, with an absolute, transcendent life, than that the disciples brooded over the meaning of the death till they came to call it life.

DC to CFDM, 1 September 1971

I do indeed hold a 'theological' theory, but not Bultmann's. I've since found something very like my view in F. D. Maurice's *Theological Essays*. Bultmann sees the Easter faith as born, inexplicably and by a kind of miracle, on the basis of the death of Jesus. I say the Easter faith was born by theological and existential reflection upon the completed life of Jesus. After all, at the moment when faith was born the one believed risen was not the mythologized Christ of the developed gospel tradition, but *the historical Jesus*, whom they had known, who had only just died.

Now the birth of the Easter faith was, whatever else it was, a religious experience. And in religious experience concepts are prior to the experience. You can't have the experience until you have the concepts through which it is to be apprehended and understood. So I say the Easter belief is prior to the Easter experiences, which express it.

Take the case of the Immaculate Conception. It's no accident that Catholics have visions of Mary, and Buddhists have visions of the Buddha, and not the other way round. Bernadette's vision in the Grotto at Lourdes crystallized and expressed beliefs she already entertained, already perhaps held, but which now in the moment of experience came to flower and took full possession of her soul. The vision is not the logical ground of the doctrine. No Catholic theologian would use the vision as a reason for believing the doctrine. The doctrine is prior to the vision, and indeed is a necessary condition for its occurrence. This is why I agreed with Bornkamm that the Easter faith is indeed older than the Easter stories.

Some reviewers say I'm sceptical about the Easter stories.

No, I'm agnostic about them. All I say is that the Easter stories are not to be taken as *reasons for believing in* the Easter faith, but rather as picturesque *expressions of* the Easter faith.

It would be a funny reason for believing in God, that I saw him take the 8.58 to Liverpool Street this morning. By parallel reasoning, what Christians believe about the risen Lord cannot be evidenced by statements like 'he just walked into the room'. I do believe that Jesus lives, but I don't think an 'event' theory can prove it. The evidence for the aliveness of Jesus is obtained by putting together the life of Jesus, the whole picture of the nature of God which the Bible gives us, and the testimony of our own hearts and our own life-situation. When all these things 'click' together into a significant pattern, the Easter faith is born – and here I quote the story of the walk to Emmaus.

I was doing philosophy of religion and not theology proper, so I wasn't so much proving the resurrection as asking what kind of thing is the resurrection, and how can it be proved.

So from my point of view your argument seems a bit off the point. It looks to me like a version of the 'beaten men' argument. The resurrection-faith is such an extraordinary thing that we must postulate a transcendent cause of its appearance. My point is (i) that I doubt if an argument of this kind can be made sound; and (ii) even if it could, I doubt if it could reach a conclusion of any interest, because the conclusion still wouldn't *justify* the resurrection belief. For:

(*a*) You have premises about the resurrection belief, premises of a purely factual kind about people's beliefs;

(*b*) To explain (*a*), you invoke a transcendent cause, namely the resurrection event;

(*c*) You then back-track and use this postulated cause to certify the truth of the beliefs in (*a*).

There must be a fallacy in that argument! The only escape, I think, is to seek a properly *theological* justification for *theological* beliefs. The Easter experiences then become by-products of the birth of the Easter faith.

By the way, another point on which I disagree with both Barth and Bultmann is this: they seem to say that if a belief is *revealed*, then any arguments or evidence in support of it are somehow unnecessary or in bad taste. Against them I say, the New Testament is a book of arguments to prove that this is very Christ, that Jesus is Messiah, that Jesus is risen. Its writers don't simply appeal to revelation or to eyewitness testimony, as if argument were a waste of time. And so I want to stress the use of *arguments* in support of the claim that Jesus is alive.

CFDM to DC, 2 September 1971

I am glad to see you clarify the distinction between your position and Bultmann's; and I warm very much to your stress on the function of the disciples' knowledge of the whole life and character of Jesus. But I still find it difficult to go along with you when you say: 'The evidence for the aliveness of Jesus is obtained by putting together the life of Jesus, the whole picture of the nature of God which the Bible gives us, and the testimony of our own hearts and our own life-situation. When all these things "click" together into a significant pattern, the Easter faith is born.' I can't for the life of me understand why *that* should produce anything so distinctive as the Easter faith. The ingredients you name (different, if at all, then only in degree) had been present over and over before, in Israel and, no doubt, in other cultures. The Jews knew all about the persistence of magnificent examples – 'he being dead yet speaketh'; they believed, some of them, in the future life for Maccabean martyrs. But what I am asking is, what could have led to the preposterous conviction that the life of the new age had been entered on by an individual and, seemingly, before the new age had arrived?

If and when the disciples have been convinced of this extraordinary situation, and if they then begin to proclaim it, calling for faith in Jesus 'crucified and raised', I am convinced that they have also to say a great deal about the circumstances and quality of the life of Jesus; otherwise, any hearers (other than, possibly, the Jerusalemites at the first preachings of all) would be bound to ask, 'But who *is* this Jesus, and on what grounds do you declare his aliveness to be *kata tas graphas*?' A characterization of Jesus is, in my belief, integral to the *kerygma*. But I fully agree that, once the story is told – in the light of the Easter faith – the whole thing begins to 'click' into place, Emmaus-wise. But it's the trigger that still puzzles me.

DC to CFDM, 5 September 1971

There is an interesting difference between us as to the sense in which the Christian faith is apostolic.

You say, the apostles had an extraordinary experience which gave them a full and well-grounded certainty that Jesus was still alive. To be a Christian today, that is, to believe Jesus lives now, is to take their word for it. Their witness satisfies me that *their* faith was well-grounded, was indeed knowledge. The apostles knew beyond any doubt, and we believe on their authority. In fact you hold the traditional Roman Catholic doctrine of faith as belief in something supra-rational, upon divinely-backed human authority.*

But I say, my faith is apostolic because I believe in the same sort of way, I arrive at the faith by a like train of reasoning, I share the same sort of experiences as the first disciples. The only difference is that they saw Jesus in the days of his flesh, and came to faith in him on the basis of their own acquaintance with him, whereas I have to read their testimony to him in the gospels. But I read the Old Testament and the gospels, I have my own thoughts about the meaning of my life *coram Deo*, about evil and suffering and the justice of God and how God can be thought through human imagery. I enter upon the story, I walk to Emmaus, things begin to fall into place. Eventually the moment of illumination which makes me a Christian comes. That moment corresponds in my life to the resurrection appearances, the Christophanies, in the gospels. The Christophanies which end the gospels are related to what has gone before as conclusion to argument, verdict to evidence. Hence their different literary character. The Christophany-story is not another episode in the story: it is a crystallization of the meaning of the whole story. After all I've read, the Lord is made known to me in the breaking of bread. On my view St Mark's Gospel is, artistically at least, satisfactory in its present form, because it leaves the reader to draw the conclusion from what he has read; and he is as well-equipped to draw it as the very first Christians, because the story, from the Baptist to the burial and the women's continuing love for the dead Master's body, supplies the evidence for the Resurrection.

Thus I argue that an 'event' theory of the resurrection belief, or rather of the *grounds* of that belief, involves a Roman Catholic notion of faith. I'm a Protestant!

Of course Christianity's new pattern transcends the materials out of which it was made. All the conceptual bricks were lying around in Palestinian Judaism: the revelation consists in their assemblage, their falling, into an amazing new pattern. Humanly speaking, the *kerygma* (or if you like, the family of versions of the *kerygma* which coexisted within early Christianity) was arrived at by partly retraceable human arguments about the significance of Jesus. But divinely speaking the outcome can fairly be called a revelation of the love of God.

*This was a tease – DC.

So if a preacher is to preach the aliveness of Jesus today he doesn't build his case on a putative and incomprehensible event which is alleged to have occurred to Jesus after his death. He preaches Jesus himself as the key to the relation of man to God. When Jesus is seen as that key, then the hearer has reason to believe in the aliveness of Jesus, *now*.

An 'event' theory might persuade me (if all my arguments against it were shown to be unsound) that Jesus survived for a few weeks in Palestine in AD 29 or whatever. But it will not change my outlook in England in 1971: what matters is not whether Peter saw Jesus alive then, but whether I see him alive now. And I *can* see him now just as Peter saw him then, though I'll use different language to tell of it.

CFDM to DC, 8 September 1971

I must protest against the Roman Catholic allegation! I have no desire, or even capacity, to believe something simply because an apostle said it. I am still simply trying to find as adequate an account as I can of the genesis of the Easter belief.

And let us be clear that the Easter belief is not the notion that 'Jesus survived for a few weeks in Palestine'. We all know that the Easter belief isn't a *survival* belief at all. It is the belief that Jesus, who was dead and buried, had entered upon a transcendent life – life absolute (Rom. 6.10) – such as at least some of the Pharisees seem to have believed would be given by God to the devout, collectively, and beyond the end of time.

Now, we are (I think) asking how this belief about Jesus was reached. Bultmann says (in effect) by a miracle of revelation: that the death that Jesus died was life and life-giving. You say, by a flash of insight, arising from the convergence, to 'clicking'-point, of meditation on scripture, on the life and character of Jesus, and on the disciples' own circumstances. I say by a revelation in terms of various sense-perceptions, which *then* gave unity and coherence to your ingredients – scripture, etc. *Starting* from that revelation, they *then* re-interpreted scripture and experience; but I can find nothing in scripture and experience sufficient to account for the Easter faith *without* such a trigger.

Now if mine is a 'beaten men' argument, what is yours and what is Bultmann's? We are all only asking how these people reached this conviction? The reason why, at present, I don't feel that your or Bultmann's account is convincing is simply that neither gives an account of that *aliquid novi* which undoubtedly does distinguish the Easter belief from anything that had been reached hitherto.

As for your entirely just objections against the fatuous argument which points to *success*,[1] of course we all know that movements holding what we deem false notions flourish vigorously. But what has to be given some account of in the Christian movement is that it appears to have had no distinctive advantage to offer or novelty to proclaim *except* that one, preposterous, conviction; and it was this conviction, tenaciously maintained, that (against their will) squeezed Christians out of the Synagogue as no other Jewish heresies seem to have done. The origins of such a situation do not seem to me to be adequately described in terms of a flash of insight, attached or unattached to its antecedents. The earliest Christian traditions uniformly claim that it was sense-perception of Jesus' aliveness that did it. What am I to do? Invent some alternative equally striking?

DC to CFDM, 9 September 1971

My teasing you for holding a Roman Catholic doctrine of faith elicited from you a plain statement that the Easter belief is not a 'mere survival' belief held upon apostolic authority alone. But in that case, how could sense-perceptions ever provide sufficient warrant for holding it? Do you not run into the same difficulty as is met by those who would argue from religious experience to the existence of God? If (as you say, and I agree) the life which the exalted Jesus Christ now lives is a transcendent life, then he is necessarily invisible, as God is, and no sensible occurrence whatever can be unmistakably and literally an occasion of seeing him. We are bound, in my terms, to move over from an optical to an intellectual notion of seeing. Seeing the risen Lord becomes more like seeing the conclusion of an argument than like seeing Edward Heath.

You might say in reply, of course, not bare sense-perceptions, but sense-perceptions interpreted by concepts and memories, gave Peter warrant for holding that Jesus was alive as Christ. But I still reply, that in the case of a *religious* experience of a *transcendent* object, the interpretative work precedes the vision, and does not follow it. So I claim that the Easter faith – the theological affirmation of Jesus' exaltation – must be, logically as well as chronologically, prior to the Easter experiences. That is why only a believer could see the risen Lord: or, to put it more exactly, the Christophany experience focuses and crystallizes the fact that this man now does beyond doubt 'see' and believe in the exaltation of Jesus as Christ.

Someone who hankers after an 'event' theory of the resurrection is (I think) bound to concede that it is possible that someone might observe the risen Lord without being a believer. Indeed it may be that he would hold that the risen Lord could possibly have been photographed. This I deny: I think that the Christophany experiences were common concomitants of the dawn of the Easter faith in many or most of the first Christians. It was the novelty and startlingness of the new faith that generated them. But a blessing was also promised to those who did not see, and yet believed. And in my view those who only believe are not one whit inferior in their faith to the apostles and others who see and believe. For the 'seeing' is only a contingent by-product of the believing and is not necessary in itself.

In mystical theology visions and other extraordinary phenomena are regarded as gratuities or bonuses which one shouldn't seek, or regard as essential, or put one's trust in. I say the same about the resurrection appearances. I don't deny they happened: I don't know. But I'm sure they cannot be made to make a useful contribution to apologetics: they ought not, especially nowadays, to be introduced into an argument intended to *justify* the Easter faith, because they confuse the issue.

In reply you say that your concern is to discover an adequate *historical* explanation of the genesis of Christianity. Clearly there's a difference between us here, in that I look at Christianity from a logical point of view, and you from an historical. My question about your point of view is, how can a historian, applying historical method, ever be justified in postulating a *transcendent* cause of certain historical events? As historian the furthest he can go is agnosticism: he must say, I can't explain it.

And I am not quite sure what you are postulating; If we say, 'Pigeons home by instinct', the term 'instinct' may have some positive content, or it may mean no more than 'We don't know how pigeons home'. So: when you say, 'Something must have triggered off the Easter faith', you may mean, 'We don't know what triggered off, etc.', or you may mean to postulate some definite cause.

Now when he meets some bizarre belief-system the baffled plain man may say, 'Well, I suppose there may be something in it.' But this admission, though it may sound polite enough, really concedes nothing at all. Similarly you may hope to persuade the plain man that the origin of Christianity is a remarkable business, and there must be 'something' behind it all, but this admission really has no content unless by a clear argument you specify what precisely you are postulating. Suppose you then specify it as the resurrection event: then I shall come back with all the objections I've made already, saying that I don't see how the resurrection event can either be established by historical method, or do the theological job it will be asked to do, still less both. The exaltation of Jesus to God's right hand is not an historical event: it's a theological affirmation about his true status. I think – though I am trespassing on your ground here – that the exaltation of a righteous man, or a prophet, or of a king to God's right hand is an idea not wholly foreign to the Old Testament. If I want to claim this of somebody my claim will take the form of applying theological concepts to the record of his life and death. People could debate the status of the Baptist, or of Jesus, even during their lifetimes; so that such a debate is not debate about a quasi-historical *post mortem* occurrence. It's a debate about a man's relation to God – is he a man *of God* or not, is his life and work a revelation of God to us? So, to end with an area where we are in agreement, I do stress the importance of the Jesus of history for faith: it is *he* who is perceived as the image of God. The *aliquid novi* to which you refer is Jesus himself: the new thing in Christianity is not the resurrection event, but the person and work of the man Jesus, who (as the gospels emphasize so often) threw those who met him into an ecstasy of astonishment.

CFDM to DC, 13 September 1971

I'm not quite clear on what grounds you assert that, in the case of a *religious* experience of a *transcendent* object, the interpretative work *precedes* the vision and does not follow it.

As you know, *ad nauseam* by now, I still find it difficult, if not impossible, to believe that the disciples had, in the scriptures and the life, teaching and death of Jesus and their own circumstances, all that was necessary to create the Easter belief. Granted that they were thrown into an ecstasy of astonishment by what Jesus was and did, something more than this is needed (so it seems to me) to lead to the conclusion that Jesus had been not merely a superlatively great prophet, nor simply a man of the Spirit, nor just Messiah (the latter is an almost impossible conclusion, anyway, after the crucifixion, without something to suggest it), but that he was alive in a unique and hitherto unexampled way, and *therefore* Son of God (in a far more than messianic sense), and 'Lord', and the climax and coping-stone of the whole edifice of God's plan of salvation. I don't think any Moseses or Elijahs or Jeremiahs, or whoever, fill that bill.

Now, in holding that the antecedents of 'Easter Day' by themselves are insufficient to account for the Easter belief, and in therefore postulating 'something' further, I freely admit that that 'something' is a religious experience (though not in isolation: I accept all you say about the importance of the historical antecedents). As such, of course it can't be proved, I agree. But I can't see why the evidence that such an experience took place is irrevelant to the Christological or theological question; nor (supposing my contention can be upheld that other explanations of the origin of the belief are inadequate) can I see that such an experience may not have been *prior* to the Easter interpretation, and the immediate cause of it. Even if no opponent of Jesus (except Paul and perhaps James, the Lord's brother) had the experience, I do not think it follows that the friends of Jesus could have reached the Easter belief without it; it only follows that none but the friends of Jesus were open to it. Why cannot a Christophanic experience be a cause rather than a consequence of the belief?

As for the point that the historian can, by definition, take no cognisance of such things, I confess that I have frequently felt a sense of unease when trying to find a formula to relate what is beyond history to history. But I still (at present) find myself saying that if a historical event occurs for which there is no discernible explanation within the historian's ambit, it is not unreasonable to give weight to a well-supported claim that the explanation lies in some other realm. If the historian is confronted by a kind of 'surd' in his story, he has no right to say that because it is abnormal and unamenable to historical procedures, he will ignore it. It lies outside his territory, but it has left a dent in his territory which might be a signal that something outside is impinging on it in an exceptional way. No doubt any theist believes that the material world is a part of a larger system: is it irrational to believe that there can be exceptional indications of the impact of the one on the other?

As for the blessedness of those who believe without seeing, I don't think that St John, at any rate, intended that to refer to believing without evidence of those who *did* see: certainly St

Paul didn't think along those lines. And I confess that I think the entire *nisus* of the New Testament documents is against the possibility that Mark was *meant* to end at 16.8!

. . . But I must add a postscript on a point in your letter I forgot to allude to earlier. I don't think I mean that I don't know what triggered off the Easter belief; I *think* I want to postulate a definite cause, *viz.* sense-communications from God, through Jesus, interpreting the past experiences in a new way: a very specific sort of 'revelation', and an exceptional sort, in that it was received by a plurality of persons, and was not comparable with private 'visions'.

DC to CFDM, 14 September 1971

I've been arguing that ratiocination comes first, and vision second: whereas you have been arguing that the revelatory vision comes first, and the theological articulation of its content is secondary. Both of us, I think, believe that the apostles had veridical religious experiences of the risen Lord Jesus. I regard these visions as logically secondary, taking them to be a by-product of the theologizing out of which the Easter faith grew. So for me they play no essential part in the defence of the resurrection belief today. But you regard the visions as logically prior: you postulate them, and argue that they are veridical, *must* have been veridical, in order to account for the church which they generated. So if you were challenged to defend the resurrection faith you would appeal to these visions.

That led me to make two different objections, according to how the logic of your argument be understood:

(i) You might be arguing that the apostles assure us that they had veridical religious experiences of the risen Jesus: we have no reason to doubt them: their subsequent careers and behaviour assure us that they were men of good faith: and so we have sufficient grounds for accepting on their authority the belief that Jesus is risen. To this I have objected that it implies a Roman Catholic doctrine of faith as assent to dogma on the (divinely-backed) authority of its (human) proposer. Our faith becomes dependent upon the apostles' knowledge.

(ii) Alternatively, you may be arguing that the phenomenon of early Christian faith is so impressive and remarkable that it persuades us of its own truth by its appeal to our religious and moral aspirations: and, being thus persuaded, we assent also to its necessary conditions, among which the chief is that the apostles were not misguided in believing that they had had veridical sensible visions of Jesus, alive again after his death.

My objection to this is that if we have sufficient theological reasons, *apart from* the Easter event, to judge that Jesus is risen, then your position approximates to mine.

You reply that, *qua historian*, you are postulating the occurrence of the Easter event as an historical explanation of the rise of the church and its faith.

My reply to that is this: You begin from certain purely descriptive premisses as to what the apostles did, believed and wrote. You then postulate the resurrection event as the explanation of these facts. You argue back from effect to cause. You then make a further inference the other way, from the cause back to the effects, namely that the beliefs of the apostles were true. I say that in history a theory can't have more content than the observations on which it's based, and which it is invoked to explain: you can't argue from facts to theory, and then deduce fresh facts from the theory. (You can do this in science, but then the fresh deductions from the theory are *predictions*, subject to experimental test; and so a scientific theory is experimentally falsifiable: whereas the belief that Jesus is risen is not so experimentally falsifiable.)

What led me to my position was reflection on the problem of how one can decide whether a religious experience is genuine or not. Clearly the problem is one that preoccupied Old Testament writers, especially with reference to true and false prophecy. I suggest the only criteria are theological: it's the consonance of a prophet's entire life and teaching with Yahwistic faith that persuades people that he is a true prophet of Yahweh, and some other man not. Inspection of his visions, or rather of the language in which he describes how God has addressed him, tells nothing by itself. The resources of self-deception in religion are limitless, and it would be hopeless to rely on the vividness of a vision, its extraordinariness, or the sincerity of the visionary. All these conditions are fulfilled every time someone reports seeing a flying saucer. What is more, the psychology of religion puts it, I think, beyond doubt that a religious vision is structured by, and gains its content from the previous life and thought of the experient. A religious experience presents no objectively given structure: it is structured, made intelligible, given objectivity by the projection into it of concepts which the experient already has. Hence the New Testament Christophanies hark back, in a great deal of detail, to Jesus' earthly life, and only someone who knew that life could have one (normally speaking).

Our ordinary sense-experience is given to us already partly structured, and gets its objectivity from its coherence with a vast body of other experience which we've had, and the structure of which we have shared with other people through language. But religious experience is different, and has a dream-like quality because it cannot be given objectivity by the ordinary procedures.

Of course religious experiences can be shared, but then there are plenty of collective hallucinations. Repeated collective visions of Mary have occurred in the present century: at Cairo a year or two ago, at Fatima and so on. That they are collective does nothing of itself to show they are veridical.

So I still argue that the only way to handle the question, 'Was Paul's experience on the Damascus road veridical?', is to interpret it in the context of his own developing life and thought, and to interpret it *theologically*. The result, my critic will think, is to 'explain away' Paul's conversion experience, but I claim that this is a misleading way of putting it. What I say is, don't argue that, 'Because we can ascertain by historical investigation that Paul had an authentic vision of Christ on the Damascus road, we ought to take the theological affirmations of Romans 8 for true': but rather, 'Look at Paul's life and thought as a whole and you will understand the part which the Damascus road experience played in his development. This gets us away from the bad old idea of miracles as violations of the laws of nature, and helps us instead to see the Christophany to Paul as a kind of close-packed argument, putting in a nutshell a turning point in his life, crystallizing his life hitherto and setting him on his future course.'

As for the startling novelty and grandeur of the theological affirmations made about the risen Lord Jesus Christ, I would say that they developed gradually, over generations, by theological argument; as Ephesians teaches a more exalted Christology than I Thessalonians. They didn't all appear in their full development on Easter morning. As for the historian, I think he (like the scientist) is committed as a matter of method to seek natural explanations and, where they fail, *not* to invoke supernatural explanations but to admit that he doesn't know, usually because he lacks evidence. What would you say to an argument parallel to yours, about Mormon origins, which argued for the authenticity of Joseph Smith's gold plates and magic spectacles?

A Final Rejoinder
CFDM to DC, 1 June 1972

To take up your last point first, I had anticipated this (as best I could) in a section actually headed 'The Latter-Day Saints no Parallel', in my book *The Phenomenon of the New Testament;*[2] and I would still maintain that the success or persistence of other movements can be accounted for by their concomitants or by-products in a way in which the success or persistence of the Christian movement cannot, seeing that it was indistinguishable from Judaism in all its other tenets (however exceptional, in degree or intensity, the teaching and example of Jesus were) except the Easter belief.

As for collective hallucinations, the ones you cite seem to me negligible, in extent, persistence, and consequences, as compared with the Easter belief, and scarcely serious parallels to the genesis of the Christian church.

Further, I am far from convinced of the adequacy of evolutionary theories of the genesis of Christology: but that is too long a story for now.

But the most important point, surely, that has emerged from this dialogue has to do with the definition of revelation – and this is beyond me. More than once, you have drawn a sharp distinction between the scope of the historian and all that lies outside that scope, and of course you are right; and nobody shares more vehemently than I your detestation of the language of 'violations of the laws of nature'. All that I am still not wholly convinced of is that it is illegitimate to appeal to the novelty, the theological and ethical coherence, and the lasting results of the Easter belief as evidence that it was due to a creative act of God. If you identify this creative act of God as something within the disciples' own reasoning and feeling such as an historian can trace, then my only basic difference from you is that I find myself driven to call it, rather, by some such term as revelation, implying that which is itself beyond the historian's purview, though its impact and results are not.

*   *   *

We agree, at least, in having enjoyed these exchanges; and, the reader may decide, on a number of other points as well.

CFDM *and* DC.

5

Darwinism and English
Religious Thought

I *Argument from Design*

Darwinism had an immediate impact upon religious thought in England, because here more than elsewhere religious thought was bound up with and dependent upon the argument from design.

The modern revival of the argument began in the mid-seventeenth century, as a response to atomism. Its proponents drew upon Book II of Cicero's *De Natura Deorum*, in which the stoic Balbus argues against the epicurean Velleius. It is often erroneously said that the English Deists believed in a clockwork universe and an external clockmaker God; so it is worth noticing that Balbus is a near-pantheist with a strong religious feeling for nature. So too were most of the English Deists.

The first piece of English physicotheology is Henry More's *Antidote against Atheism* (1652), Book II. Later on, they come thick and fast: for example, Newton (*Principia*, 1687, Book III, General Scholium); Robert Boyle (e.g. *The Christian Virtuoso*, 1690), and John Ray (*The Wisdom of God*, 1691). The fullest statement is that of Richard Bentley (*Confutation of Atheism*, 1692). Bentley's book shows the reason for the argument's great success: it made up for the explanatory weakness of atomism. It flourished in the long period during which the physical sciences were in vigorous health, but the biological sciences had not yet established their own distinctive patterns of explanation.

For example, Bentley considers the origin of the human body, asking if any atheistic account is plausible. Most likely contenders have been eliminated; for (i) it seems clear that the human race is not eternal; (ii) astrological explanations are no longer tenable; (iii) Redi has disproved spontaneous generation, and there is no reason to doubt the fixity of species; and (iv) fossils are now known to be the petrified remains of living things, and can no longer be regarded as sports of plastic nature (evidence, that is, that at the beginning of the world inanimate nature *did* have the power of spontaneously erupting into the shapes of living things). So Bentley concludes that living bodies are the product either of a fortuitous concourse of atoms, or the hand of God. The former is fantastically implausible, so he opts for the latter.

The argument from design flourished for two centuries because there was a lack of ideas of historical development generally, and of distinctively biological explanatory principles in particular.

Hume's *Dialogues* (1779) reflect the situation during his lifetime very clearly. The only rival to the design argument of any consequence was the Cartesian kind of theistic proof introduced by the Platonists and Locke. Clarke, an influential writer known to Hume, had used it (*The Being and Attributes of God*, 1705–6). But by the 1730s this sort of metaphysical theism was in decay, and Demea, its spokesman in Hume's *Dialogues*, gets short shrift. The design argument, though, was still going from strength to strength. As well as writers already mentioned, it was further developed by Derham, Strype, Wilkins and a host of others. In opposition to it, Philo suggests to Cleanthes (its spokesman) that for all we know there may be immanent principles of biological explanation. But until Philo can produce them and prove them, he is only floating hypotheses: he cannot, and does not, finally refute Cleanthes.

The classic statement of the design argument was Paley's *Natural Theology* (1802). Many writers, such as John Hick,[1] lament that Paley was seemingly unaware that Hume had demolished his argument. But, apart from the question of how much Hume did achieve, Paley in fact refers expressly to Hume's book, in his ch.xxvi. Paley needs to be studied again to see how far he did set out to reply to Hume. It should also be noted that other versions of the argument, differing from Paley and often disagreeing sharply with him, continued to be produced; and that Paley, like Ray before him, considers and rejects the Lucretian theory of natural selection (ch.v).

II *Religion and Science*

It has often been claimed that the commonsense and empiricist traditions in British philosophy have always had the merit of keeping in close touch with the development of the natural sciences – even if it be conceded that Baconian empiricism represented a very imperfect philosophy of science. The same is true of English religion. As early as the Elizabethan period English apologists were already saying that they sought moral, not metaphysical certainty. English religion was not based on an infallible church, nor on an infallible book, but upon probable reasoning: upon experience, reason and conscience. For centuries the typical appeal was to the handiwork of God in nature, and to the appeal to conscience of the character and teaching of Jesus. In all this the design argument played a central part. It was of a piece with the ideas that art should copy nature and that country life was preferable to city life, and the admiration for that peculiarly English saint, the parson-naturalist. Similar patterns of inductive argument were used in relation to revelation – the *praeparatio evangelica*, the way the divine mission of Jesus was proved, and the moral improvement which had been brought about by the spread of the gospel.

All this helps to explain why Darwinism caused such a shock. That there should have been an evolutionary develop-ment of living things was not particularly alarming. There was no sense of shock when poets like Young, Akenside and Erasmus Darwin put about such notions. Nor was it necessarily the revelation of nature's harsh face which caused the shock. And it is hard to believe that intelligent men really cared much about the literal historicity of *Genesis*, or had failed to notice the obvious analogies between human and animal bodies. No: what was really at stake was the argument from design. For two centuries the argument had been central to English religious thought, and Darwinism was a calculated and powerful assault upon it.

Just how directly Darwin attacks the argument from design has not always been clearly seen. Various myths have obscured the issue – that Darwin was a mere gatherer of facts, and not a powerful reasoner; that he was by stages obliged severely to qualify the doctrine of natural selection; that he was a cautious agnostic who could have little objection to Asa Gray's combination of natural selection with divine providence; that his constant use of such terms as *function, contrivance, selection, adaptation* means that he remained an Aristotelian and teleological thinker, and so on.

But the fact is that Darwin is Hume's Philo with the advantage that he can *prove* his immanent principles of biological explanation; and that he regarded the Bridgewater Treatise attitude to nature as positively obstructing the development of a truly biological understanding of living things. 'My chief interest in my orchid book has been that it was a "flank movement" on the enemy.'[2]

To see his point one must distinguish between design and function. A chair is designed to be a seat and is usually made to function as a seat. A tree-stump is *not* designed to be a seat, but may nevertheless be made to function as one. Function does not prove design. The chair may also be made to serve as a weapon, and the tree-stump as a chopping-block. The detailed functional analyses of the orchid book of 1862 show that what we find in nature is improvisation for a function and not design for a function, tree-stumps and not chairs. Natural selection and design are not complementary, but rival hypotheses, from each of which predictions can be deduced: and *pace* Paley and Ray, observation confirms the former and not the latter. For example, rudimentary organs, vestigial organs, and organs which bear traces of a former function are not really compatible with design. If there were an organ of no use at all to its possessor, but of great use to another species, that would falsify natural selection: but no such organ has been found.[3] In Darwin's system wild nature is not like a garden: he leaves no job for a gardener to do; and if there *were* one, natural selection would not work to produce the effects we see.

What means are there by which Darwinism might be combined with belief in God? There seem to be three. (i) There is Asa Gray's own view, which Dewey called, rather misleadingly I think, 'design on the instalment plan'. There is a kind of *emboîtement*, whereby God built into the first living things all the possible variations subsequently to appear and be selected. Against this, Darwin says it strains credulity too much to suppose that God built into the initial endowment of the pigeon all the bizarre varieties subsequently elicited by breeders; and, furthermore, that we must in that case suppose God also to have planned deformities, parasites and so on. Monod adds that the *randomness* of the variations (their being *un*planned) is an essential part of the theory. (ii) It may be argued that God, without necessarily preordaining its details, at least steers and superintends the process throughout: but the notion of superintendence is in danger of being found to be as empty as Boyle's idea of God's 'concurrence' in what occurs in the mechanical universe. God nods approvingly, but it seems to make no difference whether he nods or not. (iii) Alternatively, a theology of development, or progressive revelation, may be worked out. We set out a series of levels: the realms of physics, chemistry, biology, history, art, morality, religion. God is progressively more revealed as the world-process moves towards consciousness, the ethical and the religious levels. But at the lowest levels the revelation of God is minimal, and the process looks autonomous. Only as higher levels are superimposed does God begin to be apprehended more clearly.

It was something like this third line of argument which was adopted by the influential Anglican group who put together bits of T. H. Green, Darwin and patristic theology to make the amalgam, 'liberal catholicism'. The key figure is perhaps Romanes, and after him come Aubrey Moore, J. R. Illingworth and Charles Gore.

III *The 'Lux Mundi' Synthesis*

Romanes, at the end of his life, seems to have thought that Paley's type of teleology was now finally exploded. The method of evolution ruled out appeal to particular features of living organisms as evidence of design, and also ruled out Paley's belief that the constitution of the world manifests the divine goodness. But he nevertheless felt that he could glimpse a Butlerian analogy: God's way is progress through painful struggle, whether in organic nature, in human history, in the Old Testament revelation, or in the life and death of Christ. Faith may in some measure legitimately project back upon nature lessons it has learnt from Christ. Romanes can even speak of Christianity as the 'highest phase of evolution', in the light of which the previous and lower phases can be seen as preparatory to, and foreshadowing, the later and higher.[4]

The return of teleology is more obvious in Aubrey Moore (*Science and the Faith*, 1889). Darwin himself, it must be confessed, was sometimes unguarded in his use of such terms as *lower, higher, beneficent*, and *progress*. Moore builds on these texts, on mild remarks in Darwin's letters, and on the drift towards a measure of Lamarckism in some of Darwin's later writings. We have to recall also, of course, the unsatisfactory state of genetics at that time. The result in Moore is the familiar 'wider teleology' on which so many apologists were to build. In the introduction to the same book Moore salutes Darwin for having destroyed the mechanistic, corpuscular and deistic philosophies and for reviving an organic and teleological view of nature. Darwin has undone the damage caused by the seventeeth-century science.

Well, the interpretation of Darwin is a controversial matter to this day, but one cannot help thinking that Moore and his friends did some violence to him and his achievement.

The fully developed 'wider teleology' is evident in J. R. Illingworth's essay, 'The Incarnation in Relation to Development', the fifth in *Lux Mundi* (1889). Since the Reformation, he says, Christian theology had too often been narrowly concentrated upon the atonement and justification. But now, in the nineteenth century, the diffusion of ideas of historical development and progress through all the sciences is restoring to Christian theology its full cosmic scope and grandeur. The doctrines of creation, providence and incarnation return to the forefront. Something like the breadth of vision of an Irenaeus or an Aquinas is possible once more.

Is there anything in this theology incompatible with the results of modern science? Illingworth deals briefly with the origin of the universe, and of man, but regards 'final causes' as the key issue. 'The presence of final causes or design in the universe . . . is contained in the very notion of a rational creation.' And 'the doctrine of the survival of the fittest through natural selection' was supposed directly to contradict it. But, says Illingworth, (i) natural selection is not the only factor in the world's development; (ii) Darwin came to admit its insufficiency, even in biology, to account for all the facts; (iii) other phenomena, in physics and chemistry, suggest design; (iv) we now see teleology in an Aristotelian way, and no longer in a crudely anthropocentric fashion; and finally, (v) Illingworth appeals to the coherence and beauty of nature.

One should add that for men of that time Darwinism was only one among a great number of models of development which were influential in several departments of knowledge and areas of thought.

Gore, in his Bampton Lectures, takes a similar line. Darwin has 'not fundamentally impaired' the evidences of design in nature; and there are, besides, the argument from beauty, and the moral argument. 'Nature is a unity'; it 'represents a progress, an advance'; and this development 'is a progressive revelation of God' which reaches a climax in Christ, 'the crown of nature'. 'God has expressed in inorganic nature, His immutability, immensity, power, wisdom: in organic nature he has shown also that he is alive: in human nature he has given glimpses of His mind and character. In Christ not one of these earlier revelations is abrogated: nay, they are reaffirmed: but they reach a completion in the fuller exposition of the divine character, the divine personality, the divine love.'[5]

Gore qualifies this optimistic picture elsewhere in the same book, and, still more, in later life. 'Evolution is as compatible with retrogression as with progress . . . the facts of human history suggest nothing less than necessary or uniform progress.'[6] His emphasis moved away from the revelation of God in nature towards the revelation of God in conscience, in prophecy and in sanctity.[7] But he and his associates always thought the Darwinian account of the mechanism of biological evolution to be at least *compatible* with theism. To my mind, they did not sufficiently consider the difficulties to which, in a crude way no doubt, Jacques Monod has recently drawn attention.

IV *Retrospect*

A few final comments must be made. In the first place, assuming it to be true that 'random mutations' furnish the raw material of the process of biological evolution, it is hard to see how Monod or anyone else can be sure that mutations are uncaused events, unpredictable even by omniscience.

Secondly, some of the detail of evolutionary theory is still controversial, and it may be that there are theoretical revolutions yet to come.

Thirdly, Christianity, like many other religions, cannot be content to make a smooth transition from nature to grace. Religion is, as much as anything else, an expression of dissatisfaction with nature, a response to the problem of evil. Religion appeals from the Creator to the Saviour, from God the Creator to God the Redeemer: yet the Redeemer *is* the Creator. If the apologist labours to prove the benevolence of the Creator and the perfection of his creation, he strikes at the roots of religious dissatisfaction and aspiration: but if the believer detests and rejects nature, his Saviour is no longer the Creator. The ideas of creation and redemption are to some extent at odds with each other.

Christianity and Judaism are sometimes reproached for their ambiguous attitude to death, to work, to sexuality, to political endeavour: in short, to this world, the realm of nature. But the oscillation, between world-affirmation and world-renunciation, is essential and inescapable.

Lastly, the question of final causes still deserves discussion. All human knowledge depends upon the imposition of patterns upon experience: and unless one is an outright sceptic one must surely claim that the world lends itself more to one patterning than to another. So the question of final causes needs nowadays to be discussed in epistemological terms. We search for meaning *in* nature by provisionally imposing patterns of meaning *upon* it, testing them for fit, and revising them where they do not fit. I would want to claim that a theistic world-view is not a rigid and incorrigible patterning of experience, but is capable of continuous development, adaptation and reformulation. In this flexibility lies its strength. The Jewish faith survives where the Moabite faith has perished, because of the very dialectical resourcefulness in theology for which believers have sometimes been reproached. The Bible does not suggest that God's purposes in nature and history are easy to find out. They are mysterious, and there may be need, at times, of a good deal of manoeuvring to form any idea of what they may be: and even then, that idea may subsequently have to be modified.

6

An Open Letter on Exorcism

The text issued on 15 May 1975 ran as follows:

AN OPEN LETTER TO THE ARCHBISHOPS, THE BISHOPS AND THE MEMBERS OF THE GENERAL SYNOD OF THE CHURCH OF ENGLAND

We address this letter to you because we believe that the Church of England is in danger of making a serious error of judgment. For some years now the practice of exorcism has been growing, with some encouragement from the authorities, in many English dioceses. Recent events have brought this fact to public notice, and the Church is at a disadvantage, because it has not yet openly debated the subject. Our fear is that, since exorcism has already come to be so widely practised, a compromise will be worked out. To control its excesses, exorcism will be regulated: but the effect of this will be to give it a more nearly official status in the Church than it has had since the old baptismal exorcism was abolished in 1552. We believe that exorcism should have no official status in the Church at all, and offer the following reasons:

(i) It is at variance with the entire history and tradition of the Church of England. From the Elizabethan settlement until about 15 years ago it is most difficult to discover any instance at all of exorcism being authorized by a bishop, recommended by a theologian, or practised. Exorcism is in fact alien to the whole tradition of our Church. And it fell into disuse for good reasons.

(ii) For history shows that it is very dangerous to give encouragement to the belief that there are occult evil powers which may possess men and deprive them of their wits and their normal moral responsibility. The Church (in the person of Innocent VIII) made this mistake in the attitude it took up towards witchcraft. We do not say that exorcism is like witchcraft, but simply that the performance of it by implication endorses a belief whose wide dissemination would be a great evil.

(iii) The liberation of mankind from demonological and similar beliefs, since the Reformation and the rise of modern science, has been a great blessing. The Christian concept of the supernatural is quite distinct from that implied in occultist beliefs, and it would be wrong for the Church to suggest that her beliefs are in any way on the same level as those.

(iv) The evil that is in man is indeed dreadful, but we hold that the proper way to cast it out is by repentance, faith, prayer and sacraments. Christ's victory over evil is freely available to all. We do not think the theology of redemption implied by the practice of exorcism to be compatible with our Church's understanding of the gospel.

(v) On the evidence of the synoptic gospels, Jesus performed exorcisms. It seems that he shared the beliefs of his own time. But, whatever view be taken of this, the Church has never expected that her members must necessarily share all Jesus' beliefs – in the field of eschatology, for example, The fact of cultural change is recognized in scripture, which itself shows how a universal faith takes different forms in different cultural settings.

With regard to exorcism, the Church's practice has varied. Historically, the Eastern Churches have exorcised by prayer to God, not by commanding demons; the Protestant Churches have not practised it; and the use of exorcism in the Roman Catholic Church has long been declining.

It is, we think, mistaken to suppose that loyalty to Christ requires the Church to try to recreate, in late twentieth-century Europe, the outlook and practices of first-century Palestine. Such an attempt invites ridicule, not to mention the harm that may be done.

We urge all who hold high office in the Church to ensure that the practice of exorcism receives no official encouragement, and gains no official status in the Church.

*   *   *

The old Anglican Canon 72, prohibiting unlicenced exorcism, had been in force from 1603/4 to 1969, and was couched in very severe terms: no minister shall, without such licence, 'attempt upon any pretext whatsoever, either of possession or obsession, by fasting and prayer, to cast out any devil or devils, under pain of the imputation of imposture or cosenage, and deposition from the ministry.'

The terms 'imposture or cosenage', are very strong, implying as they do that one who purports to exorcise is a fraud, a cheat and a deceiver. So it seemed to us a mistake to argue, as some of our critics did, that the Canon *had* by implication given official status to exorcism. On the contrary, its purpose is clearly to ensure that certain things (exorcisms, 'Prophecies' and unofficial fasts) shall not occur.

Had Bishops ever in fact authorized exorcisms? Seth Ward, Bishop of Exeter appears to have authorized one in the 1660s, and hearsay reports a case from the 1930s. The recent revival of exorcism owed most to the encouragement of Dr Robert Mortimer, Bishop of Exeter from 1949–73. Other cases are still lacking, so far as I know, but a curious nineteenth-century episode is instructive. In *The Letters of Charles Dickens*[1] is documented Dickens' attempt to cure Madame de la Rue of Genoa of what she called a 'bad spirit' and he a 'phantom'. Dickens used mesmerism and was acting as an amateur psychiatrist rather than an exorcist, but the case is a reminder of the Victorian underworld of ghosts, spiritualism, occultism and 'animal magnetism', a circle of ideas which probably helped to prepare the way for the modern revival of animistic beliefs.

What of the background to the original Canon? The first Lutheran liturgies, and the English Prayer Book of 1549, retained the baptismal exorcism.[2] Zwinglians and Calvinists objected to it, and they prevailed. Shakespeare's plays, reflecting as they do a lifelong interest in mental disorder, show something of the confusion of his times. In *Henry VI Part 1*, Joan of Arc is represented as in league with fiends, and Lady Macbeth calls upon demons to nerve her for her misdeeds; but in *King Lear* Edgar's speeches rather suggest a view of demons as crazy fantasies.

In 1603/4 the Church was doubtless determined to impose good order and be rid of superstition and mountebanks. From then on, for over three centuries, English theologians commonly took the line that although there were demons about in the time of Jesus and the apostolic age, with the spread of the gospel such phenomena seem mercifully to have ceased. The first Anglican document of standing that I know of that is fairly friendly to exorcism is the essay by Charles Harris in the semi-official symposium *Liturgy and Worship*.[3] Harris himself takes a rather demythologized view of demons, but his reference to the subject may indicate that some people were already taking an interest in it. Yet as late as 1969, when the new Canons came into force, nobody commented on the fact that they contained no reference to exorcism at all.

We drafted our Letter in several stages, and a few senior people advised us. We then circularized a number of friends and colleagues and found that a very high proportion of them were willing to sign it promptly.

Controversy was heated. In retrospect it is clear that our reference to the beliefs of Jesus was too brief. Theologians may be accustomed to the idea that the culture and thought-world of Jesus were quite different from our own, and that beliefs and practices appropriate to his time cannot simply be transplanted to ours without rethinking them; but the general public is *not* used to such an idea. According to the Editor of *Crockford* (1975–76), 'The open letter stated simply that Jesus made a mistake.' That is untrue; and we had considered the problem, because Professor Moule (to name but one) had warned us of the difficulty at the drafting stage. But it was very hard to meet it without committing ourselves to one particular view of the relation of religious truth to cultural change, a difficult question and one upon which our signatories hold diverse views. For the same reason the letter does not say in so many words that demons do not exist. Our aim was to unite people in an immediate practical protest, rather than to solve underlying questions of theory.

Crockford also attacked us for not giving definite advice. But for reasons of religious liberty we could not ask for an outright ban on exorcism. We only asked that it should have no official status nor be given any official encouragement.

So there it is: whatever the Letter's faults we do not regret it. One day, the history of the subject must be written in more detail, because it does raise important doctrinal and philosophical questions.

7

The Meaning of Belief in God

I

Every morning the Sikhs recite a hymn by their first Guru, Nanak (1469–1538) which begins: 'There exists but one God, who is called the True, the Creator, free from fear and hate, immortal, not begotten, self-existent, great and compassionate.'

Daily the Muslim recites his creed: 'There is no God but Allah, and Muhammad is his Prophet'; and he prays in the words of the first *sura* of the Qur'an: 'Praise be to God, the Lord of the worlds! Thee only do we worship . . .'

Christians at the Eucharist say their Creed: 'We believe in God the Father Almighty (= all-ruler), maker of all things both visible and invisible. . . .'

Jews daily recite the *Shema'* (Deut. 6.4f.): 'Hear, O Israel; the LORD (= Yahweh, or Adonai) our God, the LORD is one; and you shall love the LORD your God with all your heart, and with all your soul, and with all your might.'

These are the basic statements about God made by four monotheistic faiths. Of the four, only the Sikh one is acceptable as it stands to each of the other three faiths; and even then the others would not accept the Sikh statement as sufficient. They each insist that God must be *named* correctly: whether as Allah (whose Prophet is Muhammad); as the Father (whose only Son is Jesus Christ); or as Yahweh (or Adonai), who revealed himself to Moses. And the Sikhs themselves further specify the God in whom they believe in ways unacceptable to the other three communities.

So the first paradox of monotheism is this: the monotheistic religions all seem to say that God is one, intelligent, immortal and benevolent Creator. But you cannot quite say that they have this belief *in common*. For each of them rigorously ties this affirmation to a particular way of 'naming' God. For example, Muslims believe in one universal Creator-God, but they insist in the same breath that he is only truly known as Allah; and to name him Allah entails belonging to the historical community of Islam, believing the Qur'an, observing the 'Five Pillars', and conforming to the moral and social requirements of Islam.

So, although in one sense the monotheistic religions seem to hold an important and substantial doctrine in common, it is more nearly true to say that they are strictly mutually exclusive, and have nothing in common. To put it in our Latin European terminology, universal natural theology and particular positive religion are welded inseparably together. So tight is the bond that two monotheistic communities can live in daily contact for centuries without one individual crossing the barrier between them. We have 100,000 Sikhs in Britain: how many of us know so much as the name of their scriptures?

There is a right and a wrong way of understanding this paradox, and in Europe we have been persistently tempted in the wrong direction.

II

When the Jews, and subsequently the Christians, came upon the Greco-Roman scene they both alike vehemently repudiated pagan religion and ritual (especially when it was most like their own), but warmly welcomed pagan philosophical theology (even when it was very unlike their own). Pagan communion rites were devilish parodies, but Plato was 'Moses speaking Attic Greek'. They rejected mystery-religions and man-made civic cults, but allied themselves with the prevailing natural theology. But though the Christians disdained the civic cults, they carried forward the pagan distinction between Natural and Civil Theology into their own distinction between Natural and Revealed Theology. Natural Theology was a branch of philosophy, developing general theistic doctrine from cosmological premises. Revealed Theology, like the Civil before it, contained the story of the foundation and growth of a community, the City of God, and aimed to validate its rites and institutions.

Accordingly the idea grew up that there are two logically distinct levels in the idea of God. At the first level it was held that, beneath the diversities of particular positive creeds, there are certain religious universals whose practice is natural religion and whose philosophical proof is natural theology – 'natural' here being opposed to what is social and 'positive'. At this level philosophers can supposedly grasp what 'God' means, and prove that God exists, in a way independent of any particular society.

At the second level the exegete or dogmatic theologian, with his scriptures and his tradition, seeks to show that natural religion is insufficient, that a revelation has been given to a particular community, and that it is necessary for the God of the philosophers to be clothed with elaborate symbolic and ritual vestments to make him accessible to the common unphilosophical man.

The two levels became in the end rather sharply distinct, so that we usually take it for granted that proofs of the existence of God (which belong to Natural Theology) shall in no way be connected with the doctrine of the Trinity (which belongs to Revealed Theology). But there are obvious dangers in the traditional European scheme. Philosophy and theology readily fall into mutual hostility and drift apart. Cosmological concern (which belongs to Natural Theology) and concern for the social order (which belongs to Revelation) have become totally divorced in modern culture, with harmful consequences. We learn from the anthropologists, and indeed our cursory glance at classical monotheism showed us, that it is of the very essence of religion that it should unite cosmology with sociology. When the two are sundered, society loses its way. And finally, when Europeans began to try to understand other religions, they fell back into classical patterns of thought. As the various local cults of the Hellenistic cities stood in relation to universal Natural Theology, so the particular positive religions (Christianity, Islam and the rest) stood in relation to the perennial philosophy. Christianity found itself being assigned to the same sort of rank as the civic cults it had once so cordially detested.

III

The paradox we began with was that in monotheistic religion belief in a universal Creator-God is united with insistence that he must be *named* correctly, and naming him correctly means accepting and living by a certain set of symbols, and a certain social order. The universal and the highly particular are fused.

So it seems that the old scheme of Natural and Revealed Theology distorts and misrepresents the character of belief of God. It needs to be replaced by another distinction, between the God *of* religion, and the God witnessed to *by* religion. For a religion is a many-dimensioned concrete metaphor of the

Divine, a *name* of God, a way in which a people articulate their common perception of the world, their social coexistence and their destiny. So, at this level, the affirmative way, religion procures common loyalty, and makes a practical relation to God possible. Through a long history of growing moral individualism this function of religion has been recognized – and reviled. Now that we fear social disintegration, we may view it with more respect. The brute fact is that society cannot survive without a public system of symbols relating the social to the cosmological, and a public moral order; and religion provides this.

But if I absolutize the collective belief-system under which I live, I fall under its tyranny. Religion is not only about order, cosmic and social: it is also about freedom. And the basis of freedom is religion's recognition of its own relativity. No system of doctrines, rituals and moral principles whatever can be absolute: God himself, God as pure transcendent Spirit, is always more than God in symbolic representation. So the *negative way* in religion leads the believer to transcend even the most 'orthodox' and authoritative symbolic apparatus. Aspiring after a God who is free, transcendent Spirit, the believer becomes free spirit himself. Religion itself teaches this, and every believer must discover it, at least in death.

IV

We picked out two paradoxes in monotheistic religion. The first was the paradox of its insistent fusing of the cosmological and universal with the particular and social, of the natural with the positive. The universal Creator can only be known by his proper name, as the deity of a particular historical community. In Christianity this paradox is expressed in the doctrine of the Incarnation: the universal God can only be known through Jesus Christ, who unites in his own person the universal Logos, the very spirit of philosophy, and the humanity of a particular man from whom a particular society has grown.

The second paradox was that of order and freedom. Religion both proposes an authoritative system of symbols of cosmic and social order, and commands us to live by them: and yet also calls us to transcend them and become spirit. Thus religion is concerned with cosmic order, social order and spiritual freedom, and these three concerns are one. They symbol of all this in Christianity is the doctrine of the Trinity; there is the universal Creator, there is the social Body of Jesus Christ, and there is the free Spirit: and these three are one, in such a way that God can only be known as a unity of the three concerns.

8

The Last Man

*This was written for Radio 3 in 1975
as a reply to Ninian Smart, who had
argued that we need a new religious
cosmology to match the scientific
world-picture*

As Ninian Smart said in his talk, 'The Universe Keeps Hitting Back', men have a seemingly ineradicable need for a cosmology. They need a picture of the universe as a fit home to live in, an ordered system which makes clear to them their place in the whole scheme of things.

So in the monotheistic faiths which began in the ancient Near East the creation story tells us how the world originated, what its basic structure is, and what are men's rights and duties *vis à vis* other created things. Two main themes can be discerned in its account of the structure of the cosmos. First, the Creator has established the basic distinctions in the world of experience: light and darkness, male and female, the rhythms of time and the regions of space. Secondly, there is a hierarchy of different levels in the cosmos, linked by symbolic correspondences, through which the meaning of the cosmos is focused down to a symbolic centre which is an image of the whole, and the dwelling-place of God. Within the cosmos, the earth; on earth, the human race; among the human race, one elect people; among this people one sacred lineage, the holy seed; and of that line, the Anointed One. Other symbolic centres include the holy place and the holy book.

Something of the symbolic correspondence between the different levels survives even yet. So naturally does it come to us that we are hardly aware of using the metaphors which link

the courses of a day, of a year, of a human life, and of all
human history. We simply speak of the evening of life, or the
childhood of the race. The metaphorical use of the human
body is so pervasive that we do not notice it unless we pause
to think out the metaphorical uses of a word like 'head'. So
perceived, the cosmos provides a framework for morality and
art which has not yet been satisfactorily replaced; for of course
since the seventeenth century the authority of the old Western
cosmology has suffered very severe damage.

Yet the need for cosmology has remained, in a way that is
still evident in popular expositions of what we now call 'the
scientific world-picture'. The story is still a creation story,
unfolded by stages: the big bang, the formation of the elements,
the galaxies and the solar system, the emergence on earth of
life, plants, animals, men and their crafts, and finally the rise
of the sciences. It all looks uncommonly like a myth of science,
which yields the pecking-order of the various branches of
science. First the universe was all physics; then along came the
subject-matter of chemistry; then that of geology and biology;
and last of all, the sciences of man. In the same order we get
the typical intellectual preoccupations of the last four centuries:
seventeenth, physics; eighteenth, chemistry; nineteenth, geology and biology; and twentieth, the social sciences. The whole
story depicts a process of cosmic evolution which culminates,
and becomes conscious of itself, in the rise and development of
an ordered scientific community.

Now, in so far as the scientific world-picture is made to
function in this way as a kind of cosmological myth, it must be
understood anthropocentrically. For that it needs philosophical
support. So it turns to the humanist philosophy which is based
on the ideas of Hegel, Feuerbach and Marx. In that tradition
the truest philosophy is the one which is the most grandiose
ideology of man. It has seemed an attractive proposition, then,
to combine humanist philosophy with scientific myth and so
produce the amalgam which is scientific humanism or scientific
socialism. But again the universe resists our attempts to make
a satisfactory home of it, for the combination has proved
unstable and faltering. The picture of the universe given by
modern physical cosmology is precisely *not* anthropocentric.
The universe has no centre, and in those vast, swirling and
impersonal perspectives we feel and hear little of ourselves.

The thought that men may be the only rational beings in the
universe somehow makes reason totter on her throne, and
men have seldom been able to bear it for long. Nicholas of

Cusa was postulating the existence of other inhabited worlds even in the later Middle Ages, before the angels fled; and we still do it. But it is only religious projection, for which we have scarcely more hard evidence than earlier men had for thinking the stars animate. The truth is that the symbolic correspondences between man and cosmos are faint now and our art shows it. The universe challenges scientific humanism just as much as it challenged the older religious cosmologies.

So we are brought up against a paradox. On the one hand we need a religious cosmology, but on the other hand the universe confounds our every attempt to frame one. If there is to be a new religious cosmology, it must not be one-dimensional, for the universe eludes capture in any single belief-system; and it must not be anthropocentric, for though we must start from ourselves we must be able to transcend ourselves. And as every cosmology seeks to relate man to the cosmos, ours should focus around a last man, a man who lives at the very edge of the world, who has the quality of self-transcendence. We get a clue at this point from Buddhism, which in its subtle spirituality is remarkably free from the vulgar dogmatism and man-centredness of too much Western thought. But nevertheless it is of Christ that I would speak, if you will first allow me to avoid the usual ways of representing his cosmic significance. For Western accounts of Christ have been strongly tied to a particular historical tradition, to a particular model of man, and to a particular kind of dogmatic symbolism. And all three must be set aside.

First, the historical tradition. Christ, in the classical view of him, stood at the centre of a model of universal history which was coextensive with cosmic history, for the universe and man-on-earth had begun and would end together; and which embraced the whole human race, because all mankind was descended from Adam. During its course of six thousand years cosmic history was guided by God through a series of epochs of which the Christian era was the last. Thus Christ encompassed and determined the meaning of the whole cosmic process. But now this model of cosmic history has been broken apart by a huge enlargement of our perspectives in many directions.

Secondly, the doctrine of man. In Adam all die. It was held that all men know what it is to be overwhelmed by the confrontation of sinful man with holy God, an experience of moral failure and the certainty of damnation. Only Christ could save men from this state, so his cosmic status rests empirically upon an experienced transformation of the self which he and he alone can bring about. But this interpretation of Christianity is intensely anthropocentric, and depends upon a form of self-understanding which is not universal, but peculiar to one cultural tradition. It too is vulnerable to the widening of our horizons which has now taken place.

Thirdly, dogmatic symbolism. I mean by this the strongly incarnational and ecclesiastical kind of Christianity which is built upon the idea that the Divine Word became flesh and as Incarnate Lord is a uniquely adequate icon or visible embodiment of God in history. He is the Son of God, a metaphor which implies that he is a being of the very same kind as God himself, as a son may be the split image of his father. And, religion being what it is, this idea is prolonged and re-enacted, in the physical resurrection of the God-man, his real presence in the eucharistic elements, the perfection and infallibility of the church which is his mystical body, the authority of his earthly Vicar, and so on. In fact there is an affinity between this set of doctrines and feudalism in a way that plainly appealed to the Emperor Constantine and the long line of his successors, Eastern and Western. For them there was much to be gained by establishing a religious system which proclaimed a historical absolute to which men must cling.

But there were always difficulties in this icon-Christology, quite apart from its political implications. As Muslims insist, it is not easy to reconcile with monotheism, and it is also hard to reconcile with the gospels. In the earliest gospels Jesus is portrayed as one who prays to God rather than is God, and whose relation to God is one of faith rather than identity. He suffers, he is tempted, he experiences storms of indignation, exultant triumph, joy and despair. He is not at all a stately icon of God. There is nothing impassive about him. He is not so much one who embodies God, as one who with the whole of his passionate nature witnesses to God.

So I would wish to set aside later interpretations of Jesus, and words like 'Son' and 'Image', and start again with the Jesus of history, an eschatological prophet, whose finality lies not so much in what he is as in what he bears witness to, and the way he bears witness to it.

As an eschatological prophet, Jesus proclaimed the general attainability of the final good, which lay just over the horizon of men's present world-picture. He accepted the terms of, he lived within and he loved a particular cosmology and a particular highly-evolved religious system, while yet at the same he mocked it by his paradoxes and prophesied its imminent supersession. He lived at the turning-point between one world and another, and he transmitted something of his own sense of relativity to his followers. It is Christianity's strangest paradox that it is the only great religion to have been founded by one who remained all his life a practising member of *another* religion. The Christian movement escaped from Jesus' own religious world-view at once, and it could do so because he himself taught his own relativity and the transience of the order within which he lived. 'Why do you call me good?', he said, 'Who made me a judge or divider over you?' His mission was precisely not to be enthroned as a historical absolute, but to be rejected. It is macabre that he should later have been used to sacralize a world-order, he who taught the transience of the world-order. An icon-Christology cannot understand, and usually ignores, the ever-present note of mocking irony in his every recorded utterance. Yet it is the clue to understanding him, for it is his iconoclastic spirit. Modern scholarship has stressed that as all men are in a sense bound by history and culture, so certainly was he too. He was intensely a man of his own time, and a very strange time it was. But his eschatological awareness made him realize the absurdity of the whole world-order within which he lived, and so his paradoxes were intended to show men how they might live when the cosmic order passed away. In *that* situation you must die to live, lose to gain.

The cosmological implications of all this are clear. The old kind of cosmology, the kind we still hanker after, sought to represent the world as a stable and fully-constituted divine order, finished and perfect in every part. It provided the objective ground for a stable social order and religious system. But we shall not have that kind of cosmology again, for the development of religion and of science, and indeed of the human spirit itself, has made it impossible. The creation theme has been overtaken by the redemption theme. There is no single way of representing the world-order so as to make of it an entirely satisfactory home for the human spirit. The ancient search for harmony between human spirit and cosmic order has to take a new form. The universe is changing, multifarious, centreless, and cannot be captured in any single knowledge-system, and so the human spirit cannot be locked up in any single system of representation. It must be free, and ready to see the world pass away altogether.

It is an old religious insight that all our knowledge is symbolic, and inadequate to the reality after which it aspires, so that progress in religious knowledge is by subtraction rather than by addition. Only more recently, in the present century, have we come to think in much the same way about our science too. It used to take itself very literally. Now it sees itself rather as proposing a series of models of a reality never quite captured in any of them.

Religion has very often been seen in the past as *binding* the believer to a certain order, fixing him in dogmatic acceptance of one particular system of symbols. Where it is so seen, one religious system rigorously excludes another. But the last man lives at the end of the world, ready to see a world-order pass away and ready to see even his own ideas of God pass away. He is free: he has the only kind of faith which is not parochial and man-centred, and his standpoint is the only one from which a truly universal religion might grow.

9

The Original Jesus

Christians have inherited a particular view of Jesus Christ, a view which is rooted in the time of the great councils of the early church. A picture of the Emperor Theodosius which dates from that time shows a figure enthroned in heavenly glory, complete with halo and attendants. It could easily be taken for Christ, because Jesus was soon to be portrayed in much the same way: a cosmic ruler, surrounded by his heavenly court of angels, saints and apostles, just as the Emperor Justinian was flanked by his earthly courtiers in the Ravenna mosaics. Christ and the Emperor became symbols of each other.

Now, whatever your image of Christ, I am sure it depends in some way on this picture of the cosmic ruler. Even the mild, reproachful Victorian Jesus still wears the halo, and the halo is a symbol of power and authority borrowed from the emperor.

Think back to the gospels of Matthew, Mark and Luke. Here, under a varnish of later ideas and editing, we find a clear and convincing picture of a wandering Jewish teacher. Isn't it odd that the prophet Jesus of Nazareth should end up crowning emperors? He did many surprising things, but surely the very *last* thing we would expect (from the gospels) to find him doing is blessing the rulers of this world – people with whom he had absolutely nothing in common.

In modern times, many Jewish scholars have studied the gospels. With the rise of the State of Israel, and the resulting Jewish interest in their earlier history, many Jews want to place Jesus in their own tradition. A Christian reads the gospels with spectacles on, the spectacles of later Greek Christian belief. But a Jew reads the gospels from the Jewish side; his spectacles are the Mishnah and the Talmud, the main Jewish books of that period. When a Jew reads the gospels, he feels a sense of recognition. Here, under the varnish, is a clear portrait of a Jewish teacher, whose parables are like those of the *Midrashim*, and whose sayings are in the spirit of the Talmud. Jesus is very like one of the Pharisees. Even when he is shown as opposing the Pharisees, he still talks like one. For example, the saying, 'The Sabbath was made for man, not man for the Sabbath', is a Pharisee-type saying which is to be found in the Talmud.

So, many Jewish readers of the gospels want to claim Jesus back as a Jew, and they feel the Christians have misinterpreted him. The Christ of the church, they believe, was a fantasy-figure, produced by Gentile religious longings and political needs, who has very little basis in the gospels, or at least, in the real Jewish Jesus behind the gospels.

Meanwhile, Christians have been trying to purge themselves of anti-Semitism, and that means coming to terms with the Jewishness of Jesus. When Jesus was taken up into the Christ of the church, his Jewishness got rejected and left behind. Anti-Semitism was the result. In the Middle Ages, in many Western cathedrals, they used actually to mock and punish Jews in the cathedral on Good Friday. They thought they were symbolically punishing the Jews for being guilty of Jesus' death. Yet by doing this they showed their own resentment of the fact that Jesus was himself a Jew, and they were in a sense mocking *him* and confirming the Jew as a Christ-figure.

So the Jew in European history stands for those features of Jesus which Christians had rejected. Christian anti-Semitism was a rejection of Jesus the Jew by the church. Perhaps the fugitive, persecuted Jew is Jesus himself, driven out of Christ's church.

The church has now repudiated anti-Semitism. The Second Vatican Council said, in 1965, that it was wrong to blame all the Jews then living for the death of Christ, and that 'the Church deplores the hatred, persecution and displays of anti-Semitism directed against the Jews.' Well, this was a step in the right direction, but it does not quite go to the heart of the matter. The problem is that Christian theology was almost from the first based on the idea that Jesus had been rejected by his own people, and therefore the Jews had forfeited their special place in God's plan for mankind, and the gospel was to be taken to the Gentiles instead.

By the time the gospels were written, Jews and Christians were already in conflict, and there is an element of anti-Jewish propaganda in the gospels. The gospels seem to exaggerate the Jews' hostility to Jesus and their part in his death. So we now tend to forget that Jesus was very like a Pharisee, that many Pharisees were crucified by the Romans before Jesus, and that (according to the Acts of the Apostles) there were many

Pharisees in the early church. If we peel away the propaganda, it is hard to see what the Jews can have objected to in Jesus's teaching. It is doubtful whether he really was formally tried by the Jews, because it is doubtful that he committed any offence against Jewish law. No doubt some quislings among the Jewish establishment connived at his death, for political reasons. But when we read the gospels carefully, we must question the idea that Jesus was rejected by his own people.

Suppose, then, we start at the beginning, with Jesus the Jewish teacher. Set aside for the moment all the grandiose ideas added by later Christian piety. Prune away the added Christian interpretation, and regard Matthew, Mark and Luke as books from a dissident Jewish sect about a Jewish teacher. How much information do they give us? Well, we know the names of some other notable Jewish teachers of Jesus's day, of whom we have sayings and parables and anecdotes. But there is no other figure about whom we are told anything like as much as we are told about Jesus. There is no one else about whom there is a whole book as elaborate and complex as one of the gospels, even after the critics have taken the added layers away. Keeping strictly within the Jewish context, and excluding all Christian additions, Jesus is still far and away the most remarkable Jewish teacher of his time.

I will give an example of how we can search out the original Jewish Jesus in the gospels. In Luke, we find the story of Jesus instructing seventy disciples to go out in pairs canvassing, ahead of him, and he gives them detailed instructions on how to work as wandering heralds of the kingdom of God. As we read, we can see that much of this is church stuff, written to encourage early Christian missionaries. Perhaps Jesus did send out disciples preaching, but St Luke, writing fifty years later, has updated the story to fit the needs of the early church. Yet very primitive elements remain in the story. When the disciples report back, they say they have been able to expel even demons. Jesus is exalted and he cries out: 'I saw Satan fall like lightning from Heaven!' Now that is the archaic, genuine article: Jesus's visionary perception of God's final triumph over evil, now beginning. That is where Jesus stands, in the midst of a violent conflict between good and evil, with his visionary certainty of God's imminent victory. 'If I by the finger of God cast out demons, then the kingdom of God has come upon you.'

This is the message of Jesus the Jew: God's kingdom is near. His sense of an all-enveloping conflict of good and evil was so strong that he, in effect, lived at the end of the world in the presence of the ultimate realities of human life. For some people, that dates Jesus, and makes him seem remote, but I think the opposite is true: because he lived at the end of time, he is for all time.

Jesus the Jewish teacher has a highly-developed sense of irony and paradox. He is a sort of Jewish Socrates, who uses a teasing, indirect method to awaken people to the reality of God. It would be quite unthinkable for him to prove the existence of God, or to proclaim himself as the Incarnation of God. He is simply not in that thought-world at all. He uses irony, humour and stories to awaken perception. He ridicules our painfully literalistic understanding of God by directing us to think of God in ways he, and we, *know* are absurd. In one story, he tells us to think of God as a lazy judge who cannot be bothered. We have got to keep nagging at him. Elsewhere though, he says just the opposite: *don't* keep nagging in prayer. The parables solemnly assure us that bad men are good and good men are bad. One story tells us to admire a spendthrift, another a swindler, and another one an outcast. The method of Jesus's teaching is to evoke a sense of God by the use of irony and paradox. His method is not literal or dogmatic, but always oblique. He uses the same stratagems against himself: 'Why do you call me good?' 'Who made me a judge over you?' He calls himself a servant, not a Lord, the very least in the kingdom of Heaven. Jesus's message was indirect and ironical in a way that makes the standard Christian doctrine of him as a straight Incarnation of God seem very flat-footed. It eliminates his subtlety.

Those medieval Good Friday rituals in which Jews were mocked in cathedrals were horrible examples of a persistent Christian tendency to misunderstand Jesus: to repress his quizzical Jewishness, his subversive irony, and turn him into a kind of cosmic depot. Jesus himself was not interested in starting a cult of himself, and it is even doubtful whether he actually claimed to be the Messiah. Some people thought he was, but he is evasive about it. And the earliest Christian belief about him probably saw his lordship and his messiahship as *future*, belonging to the age to come, rather than to this age. His revelation of God is riddling and indirect *now*. It will only become clear the other side of the end of the world.

But Christian thought increasingly made Jesus an embodiment of God in this world – a unique, physical image of God in time. Jesus's power and glory were the basis for the church's power and glory. Doctrine and art made Jesus the co-eternal divine Son who came down from Heaven, took human flesh in the womb of Mary, proclaimed himself as Saviour, suffered death by crucifixion, rose from the dead, and then, having acted out this myth of redemption, went back to resume his throne in heaven.

Of course these doctrines are beautiful and very powerful, but they have travelled a long way from Jesus himself. The famous Christian definitions of faith make no reference to Jesus's teaching. Jesus evoked the sense of God in a subtle, oblique way by his use of language, whereas in a good deal of Christian teaching he has become an absolute manifestation of God in this world.

I suspect that Jesus the Jew has now outlived the cosmic Christ Almighty, and that the original Jesus is beginning to speak of God to us more effectively than the Lord who crowned popes and emperors. You may say that I am questioning the traditional doctrine of the divinity of Christ. I do not accept that charge, for I certainly attribute to Jesus a unique power to point to the reality of God. I am just saying that when Jesus was turned into a Greek Saviour-God something was lost, something we now need to recover. And I am saying that Christian belief about Jesus should be true to his subtle way of disclosing God by his teaching.

Most modern theologians have held that what Christians believe in is not the historical Jesus but the Christ of faith, the divine Christ of the church. I am saying the exact opposite. I am saying we should go back to *before* the split between Jews and Christians, back to Jesus himself, and start from there.

10

Myth Understood

The doctrine of the incarnation states that Jesus, as God's incarnate Son, is a being in no way subordinate to God the Father. He is a Second coequal Person within the unity of the Godhead, who has annexed a human body and soul in order to live a human life. Jesus, it follows, was not an individual man but God of God with a complete human nature attached.

This account has often been criticized but, given that people wished to say that Jesus is God, it is hard to see what other solution could have been reached. Monotheism is resistant to the suggestion that there may be subordinate divine beings, so it is difficult to see any alternative but the very strange idea of a distinction of persons within the one God. Again, given that it was impossible either to convert God into a man, or to deify a man – both pagan ideas – what other solution could there be except to say that a Second Person of God annexed or assumed an impersonal human nature? Yet the effect was to make of Jesus the sort of being one often meets nowadays in science fiction – an apparently human being who is really under the control of an immensely powerful alien intelligence. The alien allows his human aspect some relatively autonomous human will and intelligence, but there is no doubt that it is the alien who is in charge, because occasionally it lets flash out the fullness of its mighty power and insight.

At any rate, from the doctrine is derived the common Christian picture of Jesus as God who descended from heaven to live among men. He voluntarily accepted human limitation, though at any moment he could throw it off. His life on earth was a unique combination of common humanity and spectacular theophany. Being possessed of the fullness of the divine nature, he had perfect insight into and control of events and knew just what he must do. He must die on the cross to save mankind from sin, he must rise on the third day, he must commission the church and institute its ministry and sacraments, and he must take his human body and soul back with him to his heavenly throne, there to reign over the entire universe.

This view of Jesus raises various questions. Is it true? Did Jesus teach it, as the Council of Chalcedon claims he did? Did the early Christians believe it? And is it an integral part of Christian faith?

I *Is it True?*

We take first the question of truth. The first difficulty we meet is that from the historian's point of view we scarcely know enough about Jesus to be able even to comment on such claims about him. Just how much we can say with assurance is highly controversial. If we can say little or nothing it is hard to see how the doctrine could ever be justified, but let us for a moment assume a conservative view of the historicity of the gospels, and see how the argument goes.

To show that Jesus was God Incarnate it is necessary to pick out some features of his life and work which are explicable upon no other hypothesis. Theologians at various times have cited a large number of such features, such as the fulfilment of prophecy in Jesus, the performance of great miracles by and in him, the splendour of his moral teaching and so on. But unfortunately all these features can be paralleled elsewhere in the Jewish tradition, associated with unquestionably human figures. For example, Moses has a marvellous infancy, delivers his people, is prophet and miracle-worker, communes with God, gives a moral revelation from God, and in later belief ascends to heaven. Another example is that of Elijah: he is filled with God's Spirit, speaks with great authority, pronounces God's judgment, wields miraculous and prophetic powers, is taken up to heaven, bestows the Spirit of God upon his disciple, appears posthumously, can be prayed to, and is awaited as final deliverer. That makes fourteen divinity-indicating characteristics paralleled in two men only! Evidently the gospel writers wished to portray Jesus as completing the great line of biblical men of God, and therefore show him as combining in his own person all their charismatic qualities. But in so doing they set Jesus in a line of men and attributed to him qualities given in earlier times to other men. In the Bible God is pictured as giving to *men* the power to pronounce God's judgment, reveal God's will, promise God's forgiveness and bring God's salvation. These great charismatic powers are seen

as proofs of a divine mission – a mission from God – but
certainly not as sure signs that the one who has been given
them is himself a coequal divine being. So, quite apart from
historical-critical questions, the arguments based on supposedly
divinity-indicating features of Jesus' life and work are invalid.

A quite different argument appeals to religious experience.
Some people claim to know as God one whom they can at the
same time identify as none other than Jesus. But psychologically
it seems beyond doubt that experiences of Jesus as God are
determined by a prior belief that he is God, and cannot without
circularity be appealed to in support of that belief. In the long
run appeal to visions and private experiences is ineffectual.
Theological claims can only be defended by theological
arguments.

So far I conclude that we do not have sufficient evidence
rationally to justify the belief that Jesus is God, and it is hard
to see how we ever could have. But there may yet be grounds
for believing it upon the authority of Jesus himself or his first
followers, or for reasons of coherence.

II *Did Jesus Claim It?*

Secondly, then, did Jesus claim it? Some argue that there is an
implicit claim to divinity in Jesus' prayers and his language
about his relation to God. Once again there are serious
historical difficulties, but let us again set them aside. Even if
Jesus spoke all these words, they would not be sufficient,
because his language is repeated *verbatim* in the literature of
mysticism, for example among the Sufis; and it is not possible
for every mystic who claims union with God to be a unique
incarnation of God.

The title 'Son of God' raises special difficulties, because its
meaning is so ambiguous and Jesus' use of it so uncertain.
Sometimes it may have a mystical meaning. Sometimes it may
be used in the Christian sense of the perfect servant and
revealer of God, who brings in and rules over the time of
salvation. But in neither use does it imply anything approaching
a claim to coequal divinity. To call oneself a son of God is
rather to stress one's subordination to God and one's human
devotion. The pagan idea that God may literally have a son is
of course quite foreign to the Bible.

Furthermore, critics are agreed that Jesus did not in fact
claim coequal divinity. The style and content of his message
are simply incompatible with the view that he thought himself

God and expected to be paid divine honours. He did not utter oracles about himself, but used language as a tool for revealing the coming and the claims of one other than himself. His whole linguistic style is not self-revelatory but God-revealing. Examination of his style shows how transcendent, holy, mysterious and yet confoundingly gracious was the God in whom he believed. His teaching style could not be more opposed to the idea that he sought to create a cult of himself as God of God.

Some people put forward the rather desperate argument that Jesus was God but was unaware of it. But the God of Israel is Spirit and can neither slumber nor sleep, so the suggestion is incoherent. In so far as people do move in this direction they give up the doctrine of the incarnation and begin to see Jesus as a perfectly God-guided man. Such a view may be close to what the synoptic gospels of Matthew, Mark and Luke say, but it is not orthodoxy. The synoptic gospels present Jesus as a man filled with God's Spirit and predestined to be the Messiah, God's ideal Son and Servant who fulfils the scriptures and brings final salvation. It seems a reasonable view of Jesus, but it is not the incarnation.

III *Does the New Testament Teach it?*

The question of whether the New Testament actually teaches the full deity of Jesus is notoriously controversial. Since most people regard the doctrine as the essence of Christianity the very fact that the New Testament's teaching is uncertain is highly significant. The New Testament contains many books by different writers, who say very different things. The nearest they come to a common view of Jesus is in holding that he is Lord, Messiah and Son of God, but all of these titles express Jesus' role as bringer of salvation and none of them implies coequal deity. Furthermore, New Testament metaphors only gradually developed into later dogmas, so that even in those places where conservative interpreters do claim to detect the orthodox doctrine it is very hard to be sure that they are not reading back later ideas into the text.

So it is not easy to generalize about what the New Testament says with any assurance. But I believe that the fairest conclusion is that New Testament does not strictly teach the doctrine of the incarnation, for four reasons:

The New Testament is not dogmatic. The concept of theology, in the modern sense, did not exist then. Salvation was not thought to be dependent on correct doctrinal belief. The early believers' interest in Jesus was purely religious, and all their language about him expresses their experience of salvation through him. The later dogmatic and metaphysical concerns did not yet exist.

The necessary concepts had not been formulated. It was clearly wrong simply to identify Jesus with God the Father, it was clearly wrong to say that Jesus was the only God worshipped by Christians, and it was clearly wrong to hail Jesus as a second distinct God alongside God the Father. So there was no way of saying clearly and intelligibly that Jesus was God until much later times, when the concept of a distinction of Persons within the one Godhead had been framed.

The New Testament is monotheistic. Although the language of the New Testament exalts Jesus very highly, there is no indication that its fundamental monotheism is in question. Thus even St John's Gospel, whatever else it says, still insists that God the Father is the only God and is the God of the risen Jesus. It is true that Jesus is connected up with a great variety of heavenly figures and mediating principles, for there were many such figures in the religious imagination of contemporary Judaism – figures like the Son of Man, the Son of God, and the Word and the Wisdom of God. But none of these figures can for a moment be thought coequal in religious reality with the Most High, the God of Israel. And we must be wary of deducing theological statements from highly metaphorical language: to take just one example, it would be rash to deduce the existence of a belief in reincarnation from the claim that John the Baptist 'is' Elijah.

The New Testament's concern is religious. To read the New Testament as trying in a loose and fumbling manner to grope its way towards the later dogmatic orthodoxy is to misread it. The old slogan, 'The church to teach, and the Bible to prove', suggests that the New Testament's only value is as a witness in support of the later orthodoxy. Yet, as we have seen, it is not a very co-operative witness and the claim that the Athanasian Creed 'may be proved by most certain warrants of holy scripture' is surely very extravagant. If we read the epistles as would-be dogmatic statements we separate them from Jesus, for no one can claim that the message of Jesus was anything but purely religious. The only way to make coherent sense of the New Testament is to break with the dogmatic habit of mind and to see the early Christian response to Jesus in purely religious and practical terms like his own. Jesus was not concerned with cosmic rank and correct doctrine, but only with salvation; and the concern of the early Christians was equally practical.

So I conclude that it is anachronistic, and in a way a corruption of the New Testament, to regard it as teaching the divinity of Christ. And if you do not accept this strong conclusion, you must certainly accept a weaker one: there were some in early times (such as those whose beliefs are reflected in the Acts of the Apostles) for whom there was in Jesus a final way to salvation without belief in the Incarnation.

IV *Is it Integral to Christian Faith?*

There can be no doubt that the doctrine of the Incarnation was an essential part of the developed dogmatic faith of Christendom. Jesus was seen as having founded the church and as having given it plenary authority. He was the principle of the church, and if he was coequally divine then the church's authority, its sole custody of entry to heaven, and its historic mission were as firmly guaranteed as possible. As the church assumed public responsibility for social control, for providing a cosmology for a whole society and for being the intellectual basis of a civilization it was as necessary to declare Jesus to be God as it had been in former times to declare that the king was descended from the gods and acted in their name.

But now that Christendom is passing away people have been aware for a hundred years and more of how very strange the whole mighty edifice was, and in particular what a gap there is between the human Jesus and the Christ of the developed faith. Jesus had been a devout Jew, a *hasid*, a prophet and rabbi, a man of the spoken word. His concern was as austerely and purely religious as the Buddha's. He regarded this present world as passing away, had no interest in speculation or civilization, and cared only for the meeting of the individual with the coming reality of God. He looked for the arrival of a new world and an outpouring of God's salvation, and he demanded a radical decision for God.

The theology of Christendom was very different from what Jesus had stood for, and its account of Jesus had little basis in his actual teaching. He was held to be a perfect revelation of God, but the ways in which he had actually revealed God in his words did not determine the way in which this was understood. The developed ideas of his person, of his work and of salvation owed little to his own message. For the first two centuries great authority attached to the oral tradition of his spoken words, a fact which indicates that at first it was recognized that his God-revealing and saving power had been above all manifest in the way he used language. But when the age of doctrinal definition began the secondary structure of beliefs about him became gradually more important than the tradition of his teaching, and so it remains to this day. Theologians still tend to see Christianity as beginning after Jesus' death, in the early church, so that it is essentially a structure of secondary ideas built upon him rather than something founded in him.

The Protestant Reformers went some way to dismantling Christendom, but they kept the essentials of its dogmatic framework and they took their lead from St Paul rather than from Jesus. They did not fully recover Jesus' own message, so that to this day the Jesus of Protestantism is still very considerably distorted, and very different from the historical Jesus. Partly the problem was the difficulty of recovering and understanding the eschatology which colours both the message of Jesus and the faith of the early Christians, and partly it was the result of the long alienation of the church from the Jews.

In modern times the main obstacle to the rediscovery of Jesus and the primitive faith is still this question of eschatology. For nearly a century it has been widely thought that the message of Jesus and the faith of the first Christians owed their power and joy to factual expectations which sadly turned out to be unfounded. Hence there has been an elegiac note in some of the best modern theology, for people have feared that the Christianity's first purity and freshness are irrecoverable. But if this is correct then theology is in trouble, for it has to be admitted that Christianity rests on a mistake, and has perforce turned into a mythical and dogmatic system of ideas hopelessly cut off from its own origins.

However, I believe the pessimism has been excessive. The dogmatic mind tends to be too literal in its understanding of the language of eschatology, and the mistake was compounded by the well-known liberal habit (strong in the late nineteenth century) of regarding exotic religious beliefs as resting upon factual errors. If the New Testament is read from a strictly religious point of view and not dogmatically then the cry, 'The kingdom of God is at hand!' is not a prediction of a future occurrence but a religious summons. As the gospels say, it is a call to repentance and faith, only the repentance must be final and complete and the faith immediate and pure. The alarming word 'eschatological', in connection with Jesus' call and the early Christian response, stands for the specifically religious, the final and immediate quality of both the demand and the response. And I believe that the decline of the old mediated and dogmatic kind of Christian faith is the opportunity for the return of the original faith in its first purity.

You may complain that I have not so far mentioned Jesus' death and resurrection. The reason is that they too are to be understood through his teaching. Our knowledge of his life is very imperfect, and Jesus' death gains its religious meaning solely as an enactment of his teaching. His death is only of religious interest to me in so far as I die with him in response to his call, and I can only affirm his resurrection in so far as I receive the new life in accordance with his promise. His teaching proclaims the great reversal, and he then undergoes it himself to become the pioneer of faith, the first of the sons of God in the kingdom of God. Thus Jesus was not a god setting up a divine archetypal pattern for men to copy; and nor was he a pre-Christian figure, the real meaning of whose life was only revealed retrospectively. He was a man who underwent a baptism of repentance, who received the Spirit and experienced salvation by faith, who himself followed the way he preached. Jesus' own message and his living of it are the concrete reality of the Christian gospel.

Thus in Jesus himself and what he shows is the fullness of Christianity – without any need to introduce the doctrine of the incarnation. The gradual rise of the doctrine at a later stage is a symptom of a certain decline of faith. Instead of the immediate enjoyment of final salvation in union with Jesus believers are offered by the church a dogmatic guarantee that if they assent to the correct doctrines and keep the rules they may hope to get by on the day of judgment. The development of dogma marks the postponement of salvation into an even remoter future, until eventually in modern times faith in it is lost altogether. The idea that Jesus was God Incarnate evolved as a substitute for, and a kind of frozen memory of, something quite extraordinary that had been in the world for a while, but gradually faded as doctrine replaced religious immediacy.

Yet Christians have always believed that the faith was purest when it first began, and every movement of reform that has real weight attempts a return to Jesus and the first Christians.

This is not romantic primitivism. The point is that when a religion lives long in the world it becomes progressively fattened out with ideas borrowed from philosophy, cosmology, politics, social ethics and the like. People come to suppose that the essence of religion is doctrine and to think that its chief task is to underpin cultural values, even where the faith was originally quite unconcerned with any such thing. So the time comes when the purely religious as a category is no longer understood, and it is necessary to go back to the roots to rediscover it.

All this happened with the Buddha. A teacher concerned only with salvation, he warned his disciples to avoid doctrine, philosophy and the cult of himself. His message was purely religious, consisting only of directions for attaining the supreme good. He knew that pure religion is negative theology. Later Buddhism developed everything the Buddha had regarded as irrelevant: doctrine, philosophy, cosmology, a feudal social order and the cult of the Buddha himself. But the original message was not wholly lost, and as the great superstructures erected over it pass away it re-emerges.

A parallel re-emergence of Jesus from the long shadow of Christendom has hardly yet begun. Christendom made Christianity the most highly ideological of all religions, and inculcated dogmatic habits of thinking which still block the revival of the primitive faith. Dogma sets God behind a screen, declares the screen sacrosanct, and fiercely protects it. But Jesus' message is precisely a call to live without that screen.

11

Man, Bound and Free

The changes in man's self-understanding which have taken place during the past hundred years have been enormous, and very rapid. They have been so great that it is now quite difficult to recreate imaginatively pre-Darwinian attitudes to the living world, and pre-Freudian attitudes to the self. To take a very simple example, John Henry Newman was a gifted early Victorian writer of intense intellectual and emotional sensibility. He was very introspective, very preoccupied with the drama of his own inner life. And that being so, it is surely puzzling to a modern person that Newman had a high degree of reflectiveness and self-knowledge, and yet was quite unaware of his own sexuality. Evidently only just over a century ago the nature of self-knowledge was very different from what it is today.

In view of the magnitude of these cultural changes it is not surprising that older ways of thinking about man have quickly come to seem remote, obscure, and of no more than historical interest. Certainly the Christian doctrine of man, vast though its influence has been and still is, has now come to seem to many people not so much untrue as obscure. It is just not clear what it means. Two preliminary comments may help to reduce the obscurity.

In the first place, theologians were attempting to set out a model, or highly general characterization of man. They believed they were expounding revealed truth, though they were well aware of important differences between different traditions, and indeed different individual thinkers with the same tradition. In the Christian tradition there was a more or less standard series of statements, somewhat as follows:

The world of nature has been created *ex nihilo* by God. It is an ordered cosmos, prepared to be a fit habitation for man. Finally God created man to be the head and lord of creation, God's image and viceroy within the created order. Man's body is made of matter, and as such is capable either of resolution back into dust, or of future glorification. Man is also alive, a living soul, in that he shares the soulish powers of growth, self-maintenance, locomotion and sensibility with the animals; and he is also a created spirit, and as such he becomes a person. He is rational, he transcends nature, and he is capable of knowing, loving and serving God. In this last capacity lies his highest supernatural destiny. He belongs to nature, but is for God. Like the animals he exists in two complementary sexes, male and female. Thus his ethical relations are with nature, with his fellow human being, and with God. He was created in a state of perfect righteousness, immortal, and with an ideal ethical relationship to God, to his spouse and to nature. But he fell, in a manner, and with consequences, which are very variously described by different writers and traditions. The essential point is that the Fall provides an explanation of the present wretched state of humanity, and a starting point for the long history of redemption. All subsequent human experience is coloured by the memory of lost paradisal innocence, the diagnosis of man's present wretched condition, and the imperative need to ally himself with and participate in the ongoing process of redemption.

The language of this summary is clearly not the language of the natural sciences. The various statements in it cannot be regarded as being classifiable into either historical statements, to be checked by the critical historical method, or empirical generalizations about present-day human beings, to be checked by the scientific method. Historical criticism and the scientific method did not exist at the time when these statements were first framed, and they were certainly not framed in the anticipation that one day they *would* be assessed by those criteria. Rather, they are statements of a more fundamental metaphysical or religious kind. One cannot apply a test, or even understand a proposition, unless one already exists as an individual person. And one can only exist as a person on the basis of some understanding of what it is to *be* a person, a knowing subject and an agent, a member of a society of persons set in a world which can to some extent be known, and be affected by one's actions, and so on; just as one cannot test the accuracy of a map unless one *already* possesses the concept of a map – knows, that is, what a stretch of territory is, what the point of maps is, and what are the conventions of representation by which the map is related to the territory. So, before one can be a scientist, or an historian or whatever, one must have some primal conception of one's own concrete existence as knower and agent, set in a world. And a 'doctrine of man' attempts to articulate such a primal conception. It is thought of as revealed truth not because it consists of a set of words which match a corresponding set of facts, but rather because it expresses the primal reality of man's estate which is presupposed by everything else that is in human life.

Because this fundamental picture of man-in-the-world is primal it can be represented as enacted at the beginning of the world, or at the beginning of the individual life. Adam is our first parent, in the same sense as the child is father of the man. Genesis represents the structure of the cosmos as established by God in six days of primal time, but you could equally read Genesis in terms of the new-born child's first cognitive development. He learns to discriminate between light and darkness, heaven and earth, soil and water, plant and animal, sun and moon, male and female. Being primal, these distinctions within experience link together the external world and the inner life: and when a theologian tries to articulate this primal self-understanding, he is guided not only by the received tradition but by his knowledge of the world and by his self-knowledge. Though he was by temperament anti-religious and naturalistic, Freud himself was led by his own self-analysis into the world of primal myth.

Doctrines of man as developed by theologians are clearly to some extent culturally relative. In periods of social disintegration, when people feel more than usually alienated from the world and at odds with life, they suffer from an acute sense of their own worthlessness and powerlessness, and paint in the darkest colours the malign effects of the Fall; whereas in other periods the mood may be more optimistic. The divine image, and man's power to know and to do what is good, have not been wholly lost. Thus the degree of man's bondage to sin, and the greatness of his loss, are experienced differently at different times.

But with all this diversity, and the vehement disputes between different schools of thought, there was of course a strong emphasis on coherence. One sought a general characterization of the human condition which was loyal both to the received tradition and to one's own generation's experience of life. And a society can scarcely live by a radially *in*coherent model of human nature. Yet the fact is that along with the attempt to produce a reasonably coherent picture of the human condition, there was also in the pre-scientific period a strong emphasis on paradox. It was repeatedly said that man is a bundle of contradictions of which no coherent sense can be made. He is suspended between polar opposites: he emerges from the earth and he comes down from heaven; he is a trivial by-product of the world process and his life is of infinite worth; he is angelic and devilish; he is rational and utterly irrational; he is nothing in the face of the majesty of nature, and yet he is greater than nature. In his knowledge of his own essential wickedness he shows that he is not essentially wicked, yet when this thought sets him aspiring after a world-transcending good, it is often in his highest endeavours that he fails most catastrophically. In the recognition of his bondage lies the beginning of his freedom: yet the purest use of his intellectual freedom, when he transcends himself to think himself as object, only makes clearer still the extent of his bondage.

Thus in the older doctrines of man there was often, side by side, an attempt to articulate a coherent account of the human condition, and a recognition of the profoundly paradoxical nature of that condition. Yet these two themes were compatible: for the essential feature of the doctrine of man lay precisely in its contrast of fallen and unfallen man. And this contrast, between what men ought to be and what they are, was not just an historical transition made long ago in prehistory, but is determinative of present experience. I would go so far as to say that the myth of the fall always was intended to be interpreted existentially, as a mythical representation of the character of human existence as you and I know it now. It is a commonplace of modern thought that the function of mythology is to articulate publicly – though often in a somewhat disguised form – the basic antinomies of existence: man and God, good and evil, nature and society, male and female, earth and heaven, death and life. Every one of the antinomies to which Claude Lévi-Strauss has pointed is dealt with in the Genesis stories, and in the Christian doctrines of man which have been developed from them. And, I believe, they are still determinative of twentieth-century experience. For one cannot but notice how pervasive in twentieth-century thought about man is the antinomy of bondage and freedom: and it would not be difficult, in our own rapid oscillations of optimism and pessimism, to find our age still struggling with the old issues of nature and society, human worth and human worthlessness, confident secularism and pessimistic other-worldliness, and so on. And this is my apology for attempting, in the last section of this paper, a brief restatement of the traditional Christian doctrine of man.

Lucretius was right: man has emerged from the earth and is made of dust. In very large part, in the structure and working of his body, in his physiology, in his emotional life and in the operations of his central nervous system, he is continuous with his animal antecedents and bears the impress of his biological history.

In animals the central nervous system serves a variety of functions. It controls and co-ordinates the organism's motor response to the sensory input it receives from within itself and from the environment; it contains inbuilt programmes of action, ready to be set in motion in response to appropriate stimuli; it is capable of analysing the sensory input in order to construct a model of the external world to guide future action; it is able to learn from experience, that is, it can register significant events and modify its world-model and programmes of action accordingly; and it is able to *imagine*, that is, to simulate or project in imagination possible future events and programmes of action in response to them.

This group of capacities is traditionally called 'soulish'. It is important to remember, since the waters have been muddied a good deal since Descartes, that soul was earlier and rightly regarded as part of nature, and that man shared with animals the property of being soulish. Animals respond to sensory stimuli, act, construct a model of the world in which they are set, learn from experience, and are capable of problem-solving and, within limits, of behavioural innovation. It is not by being soulish that man transcends nature; nor is it by having social structure, by communication, or by having consciousness or subjective experience, for all these things too can be found in animals. In the ancient language of religion, what is supernatural is not soul, but spirit; and I propose to define spirit as 'the power of transcendence'. Pure or absolute spirit is Deity, pure freedom, pure transcendence. It was not conceived until the rise of monotheism, and even in monotheism it cannot be directly known. But in so far as man is capable of being spirit, he may be described as 'capable of God'. Pure spirit, being purely super-natural, is represented as the Creator of the world, and in so far as man is capable of being spirit he may conceive himself as a created spirit, made in the image of God.

Now, to distinguish the concept of spirit from the concept of soul it is clearly necessary to distinguish two sorts of freedom.

For simply as being soulish, men and animals alike are capable of freedom of attention, cognition, experimentation, choice and action. Within the course of nature an animal can act autonomously, can think and can innovate, even though its powers in this respect are obviously much less than those of men. The freedom which is absence of duress does not distinguish men from animals; the freedom to frame hypotheses and test them does not distinguish men from animals; and the freedom to envisage a goal and set out to attain it does not distinguish men from animals. All these freedoms are soulish, part of nature, and one could enjoy them and exercise them without yet becoming what a human being has it in him to become. Many writers locate the distinctively human in 'cultural evolution', the possession by the group of an ever-growing stock of ideas and skills into which new members are initiated. But even here we must be wary. Among social mammals and birds a surprising amount of behaviour turns out to be socially learned rather than genetically inbuilt, and the rapid changes in the behaviour of, for example, starlings over the last two centuries resemble 'cultural evolution' rather than physical evolution. Even man's capacity for cultural differentiation has animal analogies, as in the development of a remarkable range of very restricted local dialects of birdsong.

The distinctively human, which is *spirit*, is something rather different. To illustrate it in a simple case, we might contrast the sense in which an Eskimo or an Australian aborigine is 'adapted to his environment', with the sense in which an animal community is adapted to its environment. These human groups are able to survive in the most extreme conditions, and do so by means of something of which animals know nothing, the spirit-world. The strains of life in this world are very severe, and can only be endured if occasionally – and especially in times of crisis – one dies to the world of sense, and enters or communes with another order of things, a spirit world. Man cannot live solely in the world of nature. He has to withdraw from it, and pass over to the spirit-world in which he finds healing and restoration. Then he is able to return revivified to the everyday world.

Objectively, spirit is thought of in rather naive terms in these ancient faiths. The spirits may not be thought of as powerful beings that *control* the world of nature, as gods, at all: they are mythical beings, archetypal and almost passive. The spirit-world is so complex as almost to be a duplicate of the natural world, and indeed permeates the natural world. But subjectively the concept of spirit can be spoken of as being already properly present. Man can only live in the world by at least periodically dying to it, transcending and rejecting the natural world and the natural self altogether. The empirical world and the empirical self are thus relativized. They are no longer the sole reality.

What is distinctively human, then, is man's power of dying to the world. Soulish or natural freedom is the freedom to know and act within the world of nature, to learn from experience, to modify and adapt one's world-picture, to set and pursue goals. But spiritual freedom is not freedom *within* the world and the empirical self, but the power to reject them altogether. The harder life becomes, the more man shows that he can only live in the world by his power of transcending the world.

The conception of the spirit-world was, objectively, at first very complex, mythical and picturesque. In the history of religions it undergoes refinement and clarification. The purest conception of spirit represents it as pure freedom, pure transcendence beyond all imagery, the absolute, or wholly non-relative and non-limited, the deity of the purest monotheism. Man's vocation, to live as a created spirit, is represented as the command of God. How is he to do this? It was originally done through ritual death and rebirth, especially at life-crises. But the purest conception of man's spiritual life represents it as a continuous ethical way of life in which, by continually dying to the world and the self, man can express in the world purity of heart, a wholly disinterested knowledge, justice, love. This perfection of what it is for man to die to the world and live as spirit is summarized in the ethical teaching of Jesus of Nazareth.

Sin, then, is bondage to the world, worldliness, the refusal to die to the world; and, ironically, its punishment is death. Or rather it *is* death, for he who will not die to the world is dead *in* the world. In the world of nature, life is oriented towards death and he who tries to save his life must in the end lose it; but in the world of spirit, death is the way to life, and he who loses his life will save it. Since man is primally a product of nature and does not wish to die, the call to become spirit goes against his nature and appears repugnant to him, and the more purely and austerely the demand of Spirit is presented to him, the more it will scandalize him, and so convict him of sin. In this sense all men are sinners, because the more purely the demand is presented the more categorically men will reject it.

But if the fact of sin is primal, so is the call of Spirit. Man cannot *be* man except by becoming spirit. Hence the call of the Deity and man's refusal of it are equally primal, equally constitutive of the human condition. Man is a product of nature, a living soul in nature; and he is a created spirit, made by God for God. Both statements are true, and all the paradoxes of human nature which we described earlier flow from them.

Man's super-natural destiny is originally and in the first place to live in the world by the world-transcending power of spirit. This is already, in a sense, life after death, and the only way by which natural morality can be surpassed. Can anything further be said about man's *ultimate* destiny? One should be cautious here, for there is not and cannot be anything more ultimate than spirit, and he who lives by the power of spirit has eternal life, has passed from death to life already. Man's ultimate destiny is doubtless the pure communion of spirit with Spirit beyond the world, or after its end: but that state is indescribable, and it is sufficient for the present to live in this world by the power which transcends it.

Such is my proposed restatement, or paraphrase, of the Christian doctrine of man. It remains briefly to relate it to science and to philosophy. The kind of transcendence offered in the scientific ideal of objectivity is modern man's greatest and most distinctive achievement: but it is liable to produce pessimism, for it reveals man in his bondage in nature; and the transcendence it achieves is purely formal and abstract, not concrete and ethical. Philosophy may seek to understand how man can be both phenomenally determined and noumenally free. It may be able – I think it has been able – to state his nature or soulish freedom theoretically; but it cannot achieve a theoretical comprehension of the core of human freedom, man's capacity for becoming spirit by dying to the world. The realization of this highest sort of freedom must be practical, and so belongs to religion alone.

12

Critical Christian Ethics

In the Indian summer of Christian dogmatism the development of doctrine was held to be like the progressive elaboration of a formal system. Theologians used the traditional formal logic to work up the deposit of faith – a set of immutably true revealed propositions – into a system of dogma. Since the church's faith was unchangeable, real novelty could not appear. All that could happen was the drawing of fresh deductions from the initial stock of premises.

Later, this model was abandoned. Religious propositions purport to refer to unchanging verities, but the terms in which they are framed are drawn, and must be drawn, from the developing historical life of men. It was therefore impossible to claim that the church's faith consists of a set of propositions whose meaning is in all respects always the same. The deductive model gave place to a model of organic growth.

In our own day, even this model of organic development has had to be abandoned. For religious history is marked by sharp discontinuities, sudden shifts in the focus of interest and the questions thought important. Each age is found to have its own distinctive flavour, to make its own characteristic selection from the inherited materials, and to organize them into its own typical patterns. Nineteenth-century theology, for example, cannot be considered as simply an organic development of eighteenth-century theology. There has occured a change in focus.

The problem of identity and continuity in a religious tradition is thus highly complex, and if this is true in the field of doctrine, it is still more so in the field of morals. We now realize this so vividly that many people find it hard to see any value in the appeal to tradition in Christian moral reasoning.

The reason is plain. In the past a good deal of the detail of the Christian moral code depended upon the current ideas of the church, its teaching office and its claims; of the state and its authority; and of the social order, considered as a complex system imposing positional duties on its members. In addition, the details of the Christian code also depended on the state of empirical knowledge and technology, and the prevailing conception of the cosmic order and man's place within it. All these things have been historically highly changeable, and never so much as in the present century, when European culture has changed so profoundly that the world as it was before 1914 now seems like another planet. It is hard, in such circumstances, to see the relevance of the appeal to tradition.

The effects of historical change seem to have been more severe upon morals than upon doctrine. We can still read St Paul, St Augustine and St Thomas as masters, and almost as our contemporaries, in matters of doctrine, and then be taken aback by their moral opinions. Why could they not see the obvious untenability of their views about slavery or religious toleration, about sexuality or civil obedience, about women's rights or social class? Perhaps the oddity is in us, in that we are less tolerant of moral difference than doctrinal, but at any rate it is there. To many Victorian agnostics Christian ethics was unassailable but Christian doctrine indefensible. To us, it is almost the other way round: we can admire the great doctrinal systems of the past more easily than the moral systems.

> New occasions teach new duties; Time makes ancient good
>   uncouth;
> They must upward still, and onward, who would keep abreast   of
> Truth.[1]

Evidently Lowell, writing in 1844, was confident that a moral tradition could be continuously developed so as to keep it abreast of social change without losing its identity. We find it hard to be so confident. Time has certainly made uncouth much of the 'ancient good' of Christian ethics, but it is less easy to see how it can be reformulated without loss of identity and continuity. It is not surprising that many are attracted to the Marxist doctrine of the historical-social relativity of morals, or take up some version of 'act-intuitionism' or 'situationism', which says that in each new and unique moral occasion we must make a new and spontaneous moral judgment which is neither guided by universal moral laws inherited from the past, nor presumes to create them for the future. The various forms of relativism and situationism amount to a revolt against tradition.

But they amount to more than that, for they amount to a

revolt against reason too. To suggest that there is *no* moral virtue in consistency, or (to put it another way) that moral judgments are not rule-implying, is to embrace ethical irrationalism and scepticism, and to do so unnecessarily. From the premiss that moral judgments are relative to the empirical facts of particular cases, and vary with them, it does not follow that each moral judgment is unique in kind and does not imply any universal rule. A brief analysis of the logic of moral judgments will make the point clear.

Moral qualities, such as rightness and wrongness, goodness and badness, obligatoriness and forbiddenness, are predicated of persons, actions, states of affairs and so on, because of their empirical characteristics. They are consequential or second-order predicates, like 'being frightening'. We cannot imagine two acts identical in every respect except that one just happens to have the additional property of being right and the other just happens to have the additional property of being wrong, any more than we can imagine two horror films identical in every respect except that one happens to be frightening and the other not. It is because an act is what it is that it is right or otherwise, and if it were in some relevant respect different, then it would be appropriate to evaluate it differently.

Some people have held that moral judgments are intuitions of an objective metaphysical order of moral essences. This suggests that evaluative judgment is quite separate from empirical judgment, because it refers to a different world. But clearly it does not. It is just because an act has, descriptively, the properties that it does have that it is appropriate to evaluate it morally in a certain way.

It may be that I fail to notice some morally relevant fact in a case, and make a mistaken judgment about it. In such a case your citing of the fact would constitute a moral argument, and oblige me to revise my moral judgment. The definition of what makes a fact morally relevant is notoriously difficult, but there certainly are such things, and they show that evaluation is relative to description. Moral judgments are judgments about actual or possible empirical things and states of affairs.

But, of course, moral concepts are not identical in meaning with the empirical criteria applying them, and a moral evaluation cannot be deduced from an empirical description. If two people, considering the same moral case and agreeing upon all the facts of the case, respond with different evaluations, it does not follow that one of them must be contradicting himself. The point is that the link between description and evaluation is itself moral: given that the facts are such-and-such, then I am *morally* compelled to evaluate them thus-and-so, and to hold that anyone else in my situation *ought* to evaluate them similarly. If nevertheless you disagree with me, then our disagreement is neither empirical nor logical, but specifically moral. It remains, however, amenable to argument, and in such a case the argument will be of a specifically moral kind.

Ethical naturalists are right to stress that moral evaluations are precisely evaluations of facts, but to ascribe a moral quality is not identical with making *any* descriptive assertion. Moral judgment is a unique kind of judgment, not reducible to non-moral terms. When 'non-naturalists' rightly stress that in judging something morally good we are commending it, or evincing a favourable attitude towards it, it needs to be remembered that the commendation and the attitudinal response here in question are of a distinctively moral kind. And when 'imperativists' say that to make a moral judgment is to recognize an occasion as calling for the introduction and application of a universal rule of action, it must be understood that the rule in question is of a distinctively moral kind. For there are universal rules, conventions of etiquette and convenience, which are certainly called for, but which are not specifically moral.

Thus moral judgment is relative, in the sense that it depends upon and varies with the way the morally relevant facts of the case are perceived by the judge. And it is also an autonomous mode of judgment, not reducible to any other. It is not identical with empirical judgment, but nor is it identical with commending, approving, deciding or legislating, unless it be understood that the commendation, approval, decision and legislation here in question are of the distinctively moral kind.

The peculiar irreducibility of moral judgment appears in the fact that when I make one I am conscious that it is a judgment that I am *morally constrained* to make, that has a *right* to govern my action, and that implies a universal *moral rule* of action. It carries with it a peculiarly moral kind of necessity and authority, often thought analogous to but certainly not identical with logical necessity and legislative authority respectively.

Thus moral judgment is both relative to, and intimately bound up with, the world of empirical fact, and at the same time a distinct, irreducible and rule-implying form of judgment. And, to return to our main argument, the admitted historical relativity in the content of Christian moral judgment need not force us into sceptical or irrationalist views about the moral as such.

Given, then, the obvious historical mutability and variety of Christian ethical codes, and the morally objectionable character (as it now seems to us) of some past Christian ethical teaching, what is permanent in Christian ethics? I offer five theses in reply.

I

The formal nature of the moral as such is timeless. Since I have not pretended to deduce the moral from the concept of a rational agent as such, I must acknowledge that there may be rational agents who are quite unaware of morality. But the nature of morality is such that once one does understand what it is, then one is bound. And however much the content of morality may change historically, the form of the moral, and the capacity to judge and act according to that form, remain unchanging.

I have said that I do not propose to deduce the concept of morality from that of a rational agent. I suppose there may be rational agents who are pure egoistic hedonists, and lack distinctively moral terms. There could perhaps be a world with just one such being in it. But then, how does the moral bind us? Is it a pure, inexplicable surd in the universe, and *can* it bind us categorically by its form alone? For consider this argument: it is the case that human societies as we know them cannot live unless they have some moral institutions expressing principles of veracity, justice, fidelity and the like. But that is a purely *hypothetical* judgment. And any normal person can be moral, that is, can understand what it is to make a moral judgment and to consider oneself bound to act on it. But that statement merely describes a capacity, a *possibility,* and refers to a *definition.* And the hypothetical statement, plus the possibility, plus the definition, even put together, are still not enough categorically to bind a person actually to commit himself to the moral point of view. For he might conceivably admit the definition of morality, and the capacity for it, and the practical advantageousness of it, and yet still refuse to be categorically bound without contradicting himself. He might acknowledge that morality has been useful in the past but urge that in the future people will altogether forget the form of the moral, because what it used to accomplish will be achieved less arduously by thoroughgoing social engineering. The specifically moral senses of 'free', 'ought', 'right' and 'good' will doubtless remain timelessly as formal possibilities, but people will never feel the need to advert to them.

So we have come to a paradox. The principle of the autonomy of ethics led us to the conclusion that the moral binds us by its form alone. The form is timeless, and to understand it is to be bound by it. But morality demands that we be categorically bound, while yet it seems conceivable that someone might understand but refuse the form of the moral, claiming that people can do without it, that is, that there could come a social order in which people have quite forgotten the form of the moral. It would doubtless retain its timeless authority, but it would be a king with no subjects any more. How can it exert its authority upon someone who never adverts to it?

Theistic ethics recognizes the danger of refining the autonomy of ethics to the point of emptiness, and seeks an objective ground of the moral in the inescapable nature of things. Now the point at which what ought to be coincides with what is cannot lie within the world of experience, without falsifying the nature of the moral. The moral is never simply identical with the natural; it always has to be superadded in a moral judgment. Thus the objective ground of the moral and goal of the moral life must be projected beyond the world. It can only lie in a transcendent, unconditionally perfect one who or which is beyond the world altogether, namely God. Since the moral ideal must be transcendent, it cannot have any infallible spokesman within the world.

So the formal nature of the moral as such, and its metaphysical ground in the divine perfection, are timeless and unvarying.

II

The higher-level moral values and virtues are less exposed to historical relativity than are lower-level behavioural rules: and in particular the contemplative virtues are less exposed than the active virtues.

Aristotle made the latter point when he said that the gods cannot be thought of as practising the active virtues, for they don't strike bargains or fight battles. Only the contemplative virtues are godlike. Christian ethics goes some way with him in holding that the only purely absolute principle of Christian morality is that which asserts that the ultimate goal of the moral life is union with Deity itself, actual absolute perfection. The primacy of the contemplative life is the ethical counterpart of the divine aseity and transcendence.

Below this level, the active virtues correspond to our anthropomorphic picture of the Deity as wise, just, loving and forgiving *in his dealings with us.* To this practical picture of God – of which of course Aristotle knew nothing – correspond the fundamental virtues, and they are relatively enduring.

At the next level down is the codified rule-morality of a particular period. Here relativity unmistakably enters, for a morality expressed in terms of rules of conduct is always the product of a compromise between religious ideals and the social facts of a particular place and time.

It is because a rule-morality is inevitably a transient compromise between religious values and the constraints of historical existence that it is so serious a mistake to regard theological ethics as a system of absolute divine commandments. There cannot be such a thing. For, in the first place, if there is more than one such commandment then the nature of human life is such that an occasion will crop up when there is a *prima facie* conflict between them. When that happens there will have to be casuistry, compromise; and relativity enters in. And in the second place, a single commandment has little meaning until we know just what conduct it enjoins or prohibits; but when it is made specific, again relativity enters in. Thus the commandment 'Thou shalt not kill' is of no great interest: what is interesting is the detail of whether killing in war, killing in self-defence, euthanasia, capital punishment, abortion and so on are or are not permissible. And concerning those topics there always has been and still is disagreement. A theological ethic of divine commandments can gain an appearance of enduring authority, provided it remains so general as to be of little practical use. But when it is made specific it becomes interesting and useful only at the price of losing its absoluteness.

Does the same thing happen with the basic religious values? St Paul's list of the fruits of the Spirit, 'Love, joy, peace. . .', is noble and seems to have permanent authority. But when he descends to the detail of personal relationships in the household and in the congregation, he inevitably compromises with his age's conception of the relations of husband and wife, father and child, and master and servant. Now clearly it is not easy to claim simple absoluteness for the concept of love, while conceding historical relativity in what counts as loving behaviour. To change the way we apply a concept is surely to some extent to change the concept itself. Thus to admit changes in what counts as loving behaviour is to admit that in the long run the concept of love itself is capable of purification – or, for that matter, corruption. St Paul's notion of Christian love was compatible with rather more cherishing paternal guardianship towards inferiors than we can stomach today. Our conception of love has become more egalitarian than his.

Values such as justice, love and forgiveness are not apprehended in a way quite free from historical relativity. Our conception of them need constant critical examination and refinement. But with that qualification, they are another permanent element in Christian ethics.

III

Arising from what has just been said, *in so far as we can recognize in past – and in our own – Christian moral judgment a lack of consistency and universality, and rectify it, there can be progress in Christian ethics.*

The moral demand for universality and consistency is based on the principle that every single human being who is morally mature is capable of autonomous moral judgment and action, and of honouring the same capacity in every other human being. The theological demand is based on the objective counterpart of the same moral principle, that is, on God as universal Creator, and on every single human being's capability of God. Thus the fundamental moral principles of Christian ethics must be universal in their scope, the form of the moral, the call of God and the moral relation to God being the same for everyone.

In practice, in Christian society hitherto, individuals have not been treated equally, but have been categorized in different grades according to sex, class and ecclesiastical rank. This has been done because people have perceived the realm of nature as ordered in grades of rank, and have thought that the social world must be correspondingly organized. Nature suggests ranking, morality calls for equality; and Christian society has been a compromise between the two principles.

That there should be such a compromise is inevitable, given the character of historical life. The perfect reconciliation of nature and morality must be eschatological. The character of human sexuality, parenthood and social organization, and the irregular distribution of gifts and talents, make it utopian to think otherwise. But there can be some progress towards equality: the terms of the compromise can be shifted. And at its best the stumbling progress towards greater equality in modern times has been a move towards realization of the Christian ideal, and towards greater consistency and rationality in ethics.

IV

The morally perfect world is always an eschatological hope, never a present fact. This follows from the autonomy of ethics and the denial of ethical naturalism, and it has a double consequence, for not only may one never be completely satisfied with the world as it is, but also one may never be completely satisfied with one's own moral standards, for they are themselves imperfect and in some degree provisional. The point is crucial.

If we study the stated ideal of the Christian life as it was expressed in some past place and time we must distinguish (i) the Christian values whose realization was being sought; (ii) the compromise with current social realities which was reached; and (iii) the way in which the making of the compromise rebounded upon and in some degree corrupted men's apprehension of the basic values. By critically examining past Christian moral teaching in this way we can take a long step towards becoming more self-critical. It is a pity that historians nowadays stop before reaching this point, and content themselves with observing that 'his thought upon this matter was that of a man of his time', without going on to raise the theological question implicit in that observation. It would be valuable to do so, because to understand how and why they compromised may make us more aware of how we are doing so. Until Christian ethics becomes critical in this way, it cannot be Christian, for if current church teaching and acceptable Christian practice are accepted dogmatically people cease to distinguish between the ideal and the historical compromise, and the eschatological drive to perfection is lost. The Christian moral life is certainly not a life of strenuous endeavour to conform oneself to dogmatically accepted standards. It is a strenuous attempt to become critically aware of and to purify *the standards themselves.* That is the sense in which the righteousness of Jesus' disciples must exceed the righteousness of moralism, and it is possible only by the Spirit.

Thus, if Christian moralities of the past were imperfect, so also is ours, and inevitably so because of the nature of historical life. Progress, we have allowed, is possible because one can become more consistent, more rational and universal, in one's moral outlook. In practice, however, progress in some respects is often accompanied by deterioration in others. It is the critical principle, the gift of Spirit, which keeps the ideal alive and enables one to reconcile uncompromising devotion to the ideal with unembittered, good-humoured acceptance of human weakness and the inevitability of compromise. Only in the perfect world will human moral judgment be perfect and human moral relations perfect, just as only in the perfect world will the divine goodness be apparent.

So the next permanent element in Christian ethics is the critical principle, or eschatological hope.

V

My last thesis is that *the ethical teaching of Jesus is the foundation of Christian ethics*. I mean here the critically established teaching, so far as it is attainable, for what we have in the synoptic gospels and elsewhere is an accommodation of the teaching of Jesus to the life-situation of certain groups of early Christians, and so a compromise like other such compromises in later times.

Many of Jesus' contemporaries believed that the perfect world was near, and they framed moralities of devout waiting and even active preparation for its arrival. He took a decisive step further in believing that it was actually coming into being, and already in a hidden way making its presence and power felt. He dared to step into it, envisage its moral order, and so passed from an 'interim ethic' to a 'kingdom ethic'.

Others have set the perfect world in the remote past or the distant future, beyond death or in the realm of myth, or outside history to such an extent that it became purely contemplative and mystical. Jesus alone brought the absolute into the present, and open to all. He was able to do so because he held apocalyptic beliefs which might be thought to make him very remote from us. But is was those very beliefs which made possible his unique moral insight, made him indeed the one who transcends history.

He was not wholly understood, and in the nature of the case could not be, so that the tradition of his teaching is very imperfect and it cannot now be reconstructed with any great assurance. His message was such that one wonders if it could exist in a critically established form. Perhaps it can only exist in accommodated form. At any rate, it is in a number of such forms that it survives, all belonging to the second half of the first century, and to a Hellenistic-Jewish cultural milieu. Critically comparing this set of accommodated versions of his message, we gain a glimpse of what he meant, and that is enough.

If Jesus touched the absolute, Christianity has been – and had to be – a string of successive forms of compromise, in which the bitterness of acknowledging the compromise has been assuaged by the deification and cult of Jesus himself. Having in this way absolutized Jesus, the church could comfort itself by fancying that it was truer to him than it really was. There was danger in this, for subsequently absolutism was extended to things in time, the church, councils, the pope and scripture, with the result that authoritarian legalism tended to replace the gospel. Modern criticism, itself a great movement of the Spirit, has mercifully undone all this, and is leading us back to a more authentically Christian outlook, which recognizes both the absolute demand and nearness of the world-transcending ideal and the touching, absurd inevitability of compromise; the 'Now' and the 'not yet'. For the modern counterpart of Jesus' eschatological outlook is the critical outlook.

The central and permanently valid principles of critical Christian ethics are then the formal nature of the moral as such and its ground in the divine perfection, the central Christian values and the demand for their consistent realization, and the critical principle or eschatological hope, which maintains in its purity the ever-present demand of the ideal while accepting the absurd weakness of the actual.

13

The Ethics of this World and the Ethics of the World to Come

Any account of morality must try to give due and equal weight to two features of it which are not easy to reconcile.

The first of these features is that morality is rooted in history, in the ever-changing social life of human beings. This is most obviously true of moral institutions and moral codes, which are always constitutive parts of actual ways of life; but it is also true of moral concepts and theories. There has been a long tradition of regarding moral concepts as if they were timeless essences exalted above the flux of history, but the fact is that ideas about such topics as justice, moral responsibility and human rights do change historically, and any particular account of them is as easily datable by a historian of ideas as any other piece of writing. Kant's moral philosophy professes to be *a priori*, but the fact is that he changed the way people think about moral obligation. He was not just analysing a timeless essence: he was innovating and bringing about an historical change. It is a lesson of its own history that philosophizing is a more deeply historical activity than it usually cares to admit, and this is particularly true of moral and political philosophy.

So in many ways the moral life, moral codes, moral institutions, moral concepts and ethical theories are deeply embedded in history; and as historical products they are in an obvious sense man-made things. Not surprisingly therefore, many people think of morality as a purely human institution, generated by the continual debate that goes on in any community about rights and wrongs, good ways to live and bad ways to live. It emerges gradually by a kind of informal and unwritten social contract. Its first expression is in terms of customs, proverbs and wisdom, but it soon comes to be articulated more systematically in institutions and laws, rules of conduct and patterns of instruction. It embodies the community's standard picture of the good life, and is transmitted from generation to generation along with other aspects of culture.

Thus regarded, as a cultural institution, morality seems to gain its special sense of authority from four factors. The first is that it is taught authoritatively to young children as part of the process of socializing them, and as they grow up the young internalize it and come to feel that it is evidently valid. The importance of loyalty to society and its standard form of life must be and is instilled early and thoroughly. Secondly, morality is closely linked with religion and law and shares something of their tradition-hallowed authority. The third factor is that a good deal in morality is quite genuinely objective and as near as makes no difference to being unchanging. For there are many things and states of affairs which are and always have been valuable to men, and many facts of the human situation as they bear upon human happiness or misery are much the same as they have been for thousands of years. Since morality expresses our accumulated common sense of what is good and how it is best for us to live together it does indeed incorporate much that is descriptively true and confirmable in experience. Finally, morality's authority is to a large extent a reflection of the entirely rational claims of the group over the individual. Since morality is concerned with the common good, moral argument is subject to criteria of consistency, fairness, impartiality and universality. It is characteristic of moral judgments that they should apply or invoke universal rules of conduct which have authority if need be to override our individual desires and preferences.

So it would seem that there is nothing specially mysterious or supernatural about the authority of morality. On the contrary, it is a readily intelligible social creation, expressing the socially-evolved collective wisdom of the community, and its legitimate claim to the individual's allegiance. Someone who asks, 'Why should I be moral?' is naively misunderstanding the human situation. He is like a person who asks, 'Why should I use the common language?' Human beings are social. Rational thought is social, rational communication is social, and rational action is social too. A wholly personal and private morality is as useless a thing as a wholly personal and private communication-code. There cannot be an entirely non-social human being. This of course is not to say that we must all be passive social conformists either in language or in morality. On the contrary, social life is essentially a changing thing. But those who would bring about change must use language to change language, and similarly they must to a great extent participate in the moral order of society if they are to contribute to the continual debate through which the moral order slowly evolves.

Along these lines, then, a secular humanist might claim to be able to furnish a reasonably complete account of what morality is. He needs to add only one more item to complete his analysis. On its social side morality is, as we have been saying, concerned to set up and defend the claims of a publicly-agreed and authoritative system of socially-acknowledged rules, rights and duties; but there is in addition an element of personal ideal in morality, especially in pluralist societies. Individuals not only fulfil (more or less adequately) the social-rule element of morality, but may also supplement it by projecting and pursuing their own personal values and goals. The various personal ideals and visions that individuals project and pursue are drawn from art, religion, philosophy and so on. They may be highly valuable, but they too are human products.

This distinction between community rule and personal ideal as the two poles of the moral life is a modern democratized version of the old Christian distinction between the precepts that are binding on all and the counsels of perfection to which the few are called individually. There is a corresponding distinction between *moral theology*, which defines the minimum standard Christian life, and *Christian ethics*, which attempts to portray the Christian ideal. But the old Christian ideals were held to be objectively revealed, though realized in different ways in different individuals. The saints may differ from each other, but nevertheless there were some standard criteria of sanctity; whereas the secular and privatized ideals which have replaced the old quest for holiness are confessedly personal projections like the vision of an artist.

So it would seem that morality is human and historical, man-made and changeable. Yet many of those who have urged the adequacy of such an account themselves admit to being troubled by a certain sense of insufficiency. Morality somehow seems to be more 'objective' than is allowed for in the account I have just given. Moral perplexity, moral conflict, moral tragedy and moral decision seem to have about them a quality of metaphysical importance which is not fully to be accounted for in terms of the claims of fact, of society, of tradition or even of rational consistency and universality, and that mysterious something which has been left out is the second feature of morality which I promised at the beginning to introduce. It seems that there is something distinctive and overwhelmingly important about the specifically moral that resists clear explanation. It cannot be analysed away. When I make a moral judgment I seem to feel that I am *morally* compelled to make it, and that it has a *moral* right to govern my action. If I attempt to define the moral in terms of such concepts as commendation, constraint, decision and legislation I find that I still need the word 'moral' in the definition, or something has been lost.

Moral judgments do seem to carry with them a distinctive and irreducible kind of overriding and unconditional authority. It is very variously described. It may be seen as a constraint exerted by eternal moral essences, or by the will of God. It may be seen as a special practical kind of necessity, or as a decree pronounced by an inner judge, the conscience. It may be described as a claim to objectivity, or as expressing a categorically binding principle of pure practical reason. The variety of these descriptions is an indication of the difficulty of the subject. It is as if in morality we are concerned with something supra-historical, though it is very hard to see how this can be so.

Many thinkers eliminate one branch or other of the paradox. Following Hegel, Karl Marx violently attacked what he called 'abstract ethical idealism', which he associated with Jesus and Kant; but then he fled to the opposite extreme and produced an account of morality so historical, social and relativistic that he has been accused – with some justice – of rejecting ethics altogether.

We seem to need an interpretation of morality that will account both for its human relativity and its superhuman authority. Many Christians claim that the best interpretation is to see morality as ultimately grounded in the creative will of God, the Maker of nature and human nature. The account that is given runs as follows: The world and human nature are so constituted that as a matter of fact there is one best way of life in which human capacities flourish most fully. It is simply the case that people will be happiest and their lives most rich if they participate in a moral order in which certain virtues are cultivated and certain moral rules obeyed. All this might be plain fact, and the basis for an ethic of nature logically independent of God. Men might to a considerable extent be able to work it out and live it for themselves independently of whether or not they believe in God. But in addition it is also the case that God is the wise and benevolent Creator of the world and men, and in a revelation has commanded men to live in the way that is in fact best for them. Along these lines many people believe that it is possible to reconcile morality's this-worldly autonomy with the religious person's claim that moral principles are commands of God. Facts about the world give morality its autonomous rationality, and God's creative will gives morality a superadded transcendent worth.

However, it sounds as if on this account God is merely ratifying an autonomous ethic of nature. What we have here is moral deism. For the Deists the world-order was for all practical purposes autonomous, and though they might go on saying that the world-order was willed by God this assertion no longer made any difference. God merely nodded approvingly over a system which had become self-governing, like an impotent constitutional monarch whose Royal Assent no longer makes a real difference, because whether or not the Royal Assent is given is now determined independently of the will of the monarch and before the documents reach him. Similarly, in moral deism there is a logically autonomous ethic of nature, and no significant moral difference is made by God's endorsement of it. There is no moral need to advert to God.

A religious moralist must therefore go further. He has to say that revelation does more than just confirm the ethics of nature. Men's ability to find out the best way to live and to embody it in virtues pursued, insitutions established, and rules followed is very imperfect. So, in order to help man, God gives in his revelation a crib. By consulting it we can clarify our moral thinking and complete our determination of the good life.

However, this suggestion adds very little. For, supposing that there is such a moral revelation, once we have availed ourselves of its help, we are back to moral deism. The authority of the revelation is only temporary. Once it has taught us what it has to teach, it can bow out gracefully with its work done. John Stuart Mill once made precisely that point. A humanist morality may indeed acknowledge an historical debt to the old religious tradition. However, Mill points out that the Bible contains bad moral teaching as well as good, and if we remain under its authority the bad will corrupt the good. But if we read it with an alert conscience we can gratefully take what is good, thank the teacher, and send him on his way. That is morally the best way to learn from a moral revelation. So we revert to moral deism.

The religious moralist will try again. He will say that if the moral order is ultimately grounded in the creative will of God – which in turn expresses God's eternal nature – then the

morally serious person is assured of an ultimate coherence and
unity in the moral life. The supreme good is one. The moral life
is not a heroic rearguard action, fought largely in the dark and
full of tragic contradictions, against a basically indifferent
universe. On the contrary, it is *sustained* and it is ultimately
coherent.

On this account many of the facts of moral experience, the
general shape of the moral order, and even to a large extent its
logical autonomy will once again be agreed between believers
and unbelievers. But the believers have the advantage of a
more unified conception of the good and a more optimistic and
hopeful view of the moral life.

However the fact that believers have a certain psychological
advantage is not in itself any reason for thinking them right. In
reply, it may be claimed that the belief that God is the
imponent of the moral order is not merely psychologically
advantageous, but morally beneficial too. If the existence of
God cannot be proved or disproved theoretically, and yet one
must live upon some hypothesis, then why should we not live
upon the most morally beneficial hypothesis? The best life is a
life lived in the belief that the moral order is God-given, reflects
something of the divine unity and perfection, and is upheld by
God. This moral faith cannot be theoretically disproved, and it
has practical benefits. The believer may in addition claim that
it is confirmed by relevation.

This position marks only a very limited advance on moral
deism. It is still supposed that there is an autonomous ethic of
nature, but now we are told that certain theological postulates
brought in to endorse it cannot be shown to be false and have
morally beneficial effects where they are believed to be true.
What is more, we know we ought to believe them. So morality
is human and there is an autonomous ethic of nature, but at
the same time morality owes its special sense of authority to
the fact that it is founded in the will of the Author of nature.
We all recognize this, and so we all have an implicit moral faith
in God, which revelation can confirm.

Yet God on this account is still being introduced to validate
a fundamentally autonomous ethic of nature. And there are
many objections to the whole view of the relation of God to
morality that I have been describing.

The idea that there is a universal natural morality
establishable by unassisted human reason and cross-culturally
universal is linked with the corresponding claim that there is a
universal natural religion underlying the various positive

religions. But in fact all religions are positive, and similarly all moralities are tied to particular historically-developing cultural traditions and views of life. Students of religion reckon it to be virtually impossible to produce a universal definition of religion valid for all periods and places. Similarly, any list of the principles of a truly universal natural morality would have to be so general as to be of little interest. The moral order in society is such an imperfect and variable thing that divine and immutable authority can only plausibly be claimed for its most general principles.

What might these absolute principles of morality be? They could only be such principles as 'Be loyal to the society to which you belong', 'Do good and avoid evil', 'Return good for good' and 'Do not inflict evil gratuitously.' If such principles as these are alone supposed to be universal, absolute, evident to reason and also commanded by God, then it ought to be the case that it is to them alone that the special and distinctively moral sense of sacred authority attaches. A moral judgment would have that special quality of sacred authoritativeness in so far as it embodied one of these principles. But in fact the principles I have just quoted are vapid and almost tautologous, and do not evoke any strong moral feelings. Our deepest moral admiration and indignation are kindled at far more particular and specific levels, and often at moments when precedent, revelation and universal principles give the *least* guidance. Thus we may well admire greatly those nineteenth-century pioneers who struggled to free women from the bondage to which God, nature and the universal consent of mankind had seemingly consigned them. This long battle has been experienced by women as being in issue after issue a struggle *against* a conservative natural-law ethic of creation, *against* a human social morality which represented itself as divinely validated.

The attempt to ground the authority of morality in the creative will of God now seems to be a survival from the traditional societies of the past, which believed that the cosmos was first established as a harmonious divine order, and that the principles of morality were somehow built in from the outset by God and continue thereafter unchanged.

With this view went the claim that there is a discernible moral providence at work in the world. The idea was that although human morality is to some extent enforced by the sanctions of law, public opinion and conscience, these sanctions by themselves are insufficient to maintain the moral order. The moral order is also enforced on a cosmic scale by God's moral providence, rewarding the good and punishing the wicked. Since God is omnipotent and omniscient his enforcement of the moral order is infallibly just and thorough. It may grind slowly, but it grinds exceeding small.

The belief that the human moral order is backed up by a divine and cosmic moral order presupposes that the moral principles God enforces are just the same as those of human morality. This looks very like a projection into the heavens of the authority of the king, public opinion and conscience. Ever since the author of Job protested against the Deuteronomic doctrine of providence it has been the target of sharp religious criticism for its anthropomorphism, its penal view of morality, and its disregard of the problem of evil. Apologists for it, like Joseph Butler, have always had to argue in two opposite directions at once, for they have said *both* that God's moral providence is just enough apparent in this life to be believed in, *and* that it is so imperfect that we must look to a Last Judgment and a better world to see things put right. As Butler's case shows, the argument eventually becomes so fine-spun that it does not establish anything. The only virtue that is reliably rewarded in this life is prudence, and prudence is rewarded only in a tautologous sense, for it is in fact a sober recognition that we must be realistic and look after ourselves without expecting to be bailed out.

In addition to this, the claim that there is a permanent natural moral law built in to the scheme of things by God has always faced the difficulty that the Old Testament itself recognizes the fact of historical change in morality. Did the God of the Bible at one time bless polygamists and then decide upon a change of policy? The policy change is nowhere announced.

Some claim that the old natural-law tradition in ethics is still not quite dead in spite of the fact that our picture of the cosmos is now evolutionary and our picture of man historical. But I suggest that if it is not to fall into manifest absurdities it must be qualified to the point of emptiness. The supposed universal and absolute principles of natural morality have to be stated in such general terms that they amount in the end to no more than the assertion that moral judgments are subject to formal criteria of universality, consistency and the like. Historical change in the human condition does take place, to such an extent that major moral innovations can and do occur, and when they occur they appear to be rebellions against everything that has hitherto seemed natural, immutable and divinely ordained.

This fact, that morality develops, reminds us that one of the most important topics on which we pronounce moral judgment is moral judgment itself. As the moral theologians say, one must distinguish between the claim that conscience must always be obeyed, which is tautologously true, and the assertion that conscience is infallible, which is false. For, on the contrary, conscience needs continual education. God should not be invoked to guarantee our present moral judgments and our present moral order, because in so far as God is thus invoked, morality is frozen. The world is not already a fully constituted and perfect natural-moral order. To say so would kill the spirit of moral aspiration and moral progress. Thus the only morally acceptable way of connecting religion with morality is to regard God not as validating and fixing our present moral ideals and standards, but as inspiring continual dissatisfaction with them and criticism of them. The morally perfect world, in which what is and what ought to be coincide, must be regarded as a history-transcending ideal which lies, as it were, in the future as an object of aspiration, not in the past as a golden age from which the present world is fallen. There never was such a golden age.

So I am calling for a shift in the way in which we perceive the relation of God to morality. It is a shift from the ethics of creation to the ethics of redemption. God does not validate human morality, but confounds it by revealing an absolute ideal which inspires continual discontent and moral aspiration. The element of sacred authoritativeness in morality is best interpreted as what theologians call an eschatological demand.

Incidentally, the Torah of Moses is often thought of as the moral code of a very remote patriarchal and agricultural people, transmitted by tradition as sacred and immutable, but experienced today as restrictive because our moral perceptions have changed so much during the past twenty-five centuries. For the orthodox Jew however, and from the religious point of view, the Torah was itself an eschatological ideal, a standard of perfection whose realization lay ahead, and which was a call to the future rather than a recall to the past. If Israel were ever to keep the Torah for a single day, it was said, the kingdom of God would come. It is not quite itself the kingdom ethic, but is was believed to be ethic that would bring the kingdom.

However, the Torah's ability to function as an absolute ethical ideal is now limited, or so I believe, because it manifestly is tied to a particular society and its form of life. Large tracts of it are obsolete. As we read it, we find that, like John Stuart Mill, we are judging it, picking and choosing, finding parts of it crude and barbarous, and parts of it noble and precious. It is not inexhaustible.

But there is a moral revelation which, as I believe, does have a divine inexhaustibility. It does not fix the basic moral concepts, it does not provide systematic criteria for moral reasoning, and it does not provide a code of law. Rather, it shows the moral ideal, the kingdom of God, in an indirect way by a satirical attack on the calculations of human morality and the comical inadequacy of its conceptions of righteousness, love, mercy, forgiveness and justice. Its aim is to awaken moral imagination and moral aspiration, and to prompt us to repentance and faith. The connection between God and morality is not given in the present world-order, but is something to be sought for in a new world that is yet to come. That new world is not remote: although transcendent, mysterious and unspecifiable it is yet close, imperative and confounding. It must be decided for and can be appropriated now. I know God in the moral life in so far as I live by an absolute ideal which continually judges and inspires me, which is indeed unfulfillable and transcendent, and for that very reason inexhaustibly powerful.

I am speaking, of course, of Jesus' proclamation of the kingdom of God. Jesus' message is extraordinarily difficult to grasp, partly because of its very nature, and partly because we do not have it in quite the form in which he delivered it. As it is presented in the synoptic gospels it has been adapted to the requirements of early Christian communities some decades after his death. It had been amplified with elements of Jewish ethics and Christian ecclesiastical ethics which in many points seem out of harmony with the original message. However, if we attend closely to the oldest elements in the tradition of Jesus' sayings and parables we can still make out something of what he meant.

Monotheistic faith at its best was always eschatological. The world is not yet wholly God's, and the human moral order does not yet fully reveal the divine nature. Faith looks forward to an ideal future state of the world in which God will be perfectly revealed in the world-order and in human life. As prophet of the kingdom of God Jesus was wholly absorbed by his vision of that final state of things which for him was the supreme reality. He used various kinds of symbolic action to reveal it. He held ceremonial feasts to enact its presence. His healings and exorcisms were victories over evil forces opposed to it and anticipations of the universal restoration that it would bring. His choice of twelve followers to symbolize the tribes of Israel was also a deliberate prophetic actualization of the coming supreme good. By actions like these Jesus showed that the supreme good was not for him an apocalyptic catastrophe whose occurrence was quite independent of any human action. On the contrary, his prophetic action literally anticipated it, or seized it in advance, and displayed its powers.

The sayings and parables similarly show that the supreme good is very close. It utterly confounds the present moral and ritual order – *even though* Jesus as an orthodox Jew regarded that order as in some sense God-given – and it demands a complete break. One can and must decide for the new world and seize it now.

Yet Jesus does not specify what the new world is. What he does instead is take the traditional Jewish moral and religious values – values such as justice, mercy, covenant-brotherhood, forgiveness, piety, prudence, compassion for the unfortunate and the outcast and so on – and tell stories about them. In the stories these traditional virtues and values are forced to such superhuman heights as to produce a disclosure of the divine perfection. The absolute moral ideal, of a human social order which perfectly embodies the divine perfection, is thus shown as infinitely surpassing merely human standards of forgiveness, justice and the like.

This is, I suggest, the only kind of moral revelation that can be permanently and inexhaustibly authoritative without becoming restrictive. It shows, without specifying it in detail, a transcendent ideal which will inspire as long as history lasts. St Paul began the work of accommodating the ideal to historical circumstance. The kingdom ethic, so accommodated, becomes a church ethic. It is an accommodation that has to be made, and continually remade, for all such accommodations are imperfect and transient. Hence Paul is inevitably dated, as Jesus is not; but Paul is not to be blamed for the fact that he had the humbler task.

We began this discussion by saying that morality is embedded in the flux of human history and yet has about it something irreducible and unconditionally authoritative. The problem is to do justice to both these features of moral experience. I have argued that the attempt to ground the human moral order in the creative will of God is not a satisfactory resolution of the paradox. Changes in our general view of the world, together with the cluster of issues we call the problem of evil, have made it seem highly implausible. Furthermore, it is religiously objectionable, for it uses God to validate the merely human.

My alternative interpretation of moral experience is indebted to the teaching of Jesus of Nazareth. We must recognize that the human moral order is indeed merely human, but also that it is continually challenged by the absolute moral ideal. This ideal is best represented as something transcendent and unspecifiable which is yet near, imperative and confounding. It is experienced as a mocking judgment upon the absurd inadequacy of human moral ideals and as a call to absolute perfection. It cannot be realized in history as we know it, but it inspires continual moral criticism and aspiration. Here and there in human history (and, for the Christian, most of all in the brief career of Jesus) we see revelatory moral innovations which promise that the absolute ideal will be realized and can be anticipated. But actual human moralities, including all the historical forms that Christian morality has taken, are all of them more or less clumsy and inadequate compromises. We all have to make such a compromise for ourselves. It cannot be helped. It is still more important, though, that we should not lose sight of the absolute ideal, for it and it alone has the power to give ultimate worth to the moral life.

The ethics of creation fixed man in his place in a world that was perceived as being already (in principle, at least) a finished and perfect divine order. In the ethics of redemption we have a critique of the present world-order and a summons to a new world. The new world is a transcendent and divine reality, but it is not wholly beyond our reach. One must decide for it and one can anticipate it now.

Notes

2. Transplanting the Heart

1. S. Kierkegaard, *For Self-Examination*, trans, W. Lowrie, OUP 1941, p. 210.

2. Pius XII, *Discorsi al Medici*, Rome 1959, pp. 608–18; French translation in *Law and Ethics of Transplantation*, ed. G. E. W. Wolstenholme and M. O'Connor, Ciba Foundation Blueprint 1968, Appendix 4. Medical reflections on the twilight zone in G. Biörck, 'When is Death?', *Wisconsin Law Review* 1968, no. 2, pp. 484–97.

3. A thorough study by J. G. Castel, 'Some Legal aspects of Organ Transplantation in Canada' has appeared in the *Canadian Bar Review*, vol. XLVI, no. 3, September 1968, pp. 345–405. The American scene is surveyed in A. M. Sadler Jr. and B. L. Sadler, 'Transplantation and the Law', in the *Georgetown Law Journal* 57, no. 1, 1968, pp. 5ff.

4. For a 'no nonsense' humanist on this, see Henry Miller, 'New Doctors' Dilemmas', *Encounter* XXXII no. 3, March 1969, pp. 25ff.

5. Zoologist already endure legal controls upon experiments with animals. Legislation on cruelty to animals similarly came much earlier than legislation on cruelty to children!

3. The Language of Eschatology: F. D. Maurice's Treatment of Heaven and Hell

1. Frederick Maurice, *The Life of Frederick Denison Maurice*, 4th ed., Macmillan 1885, vol. I, pp. 132f.

2. Robert Jenkin, *The Reasonableness and Certainty of the Christian Religion*, 4th ed., London 1715, vol. II, pp. 423–35.

3. George Berkeley, *Works*, ed. A. A. Luce and T. E. Jessop, Nelson 1959, vol. III, p. 297. The words are those of Berkeley's character Euphranor, but represent the author's own views.

4. F. D. Maurice, *The New Statute and Mr Ward*, Oxford 1945, pp. 19–21; *Life* I, pp. 396–8 (my italics).

5. Jonathan Edwards, *Select Works*, The Banner of Truth Trust, London 1959, vol. II, p. 191.

6. F. D. Maurice, *Theological Essays*, 3rd ed., Macmillan 1871, p. 480.

7. F. D. Maurice, *The Word 'Eternal' and the Punishment of the Wicked*, Macmillan, Cambridge 1854, p. 36.

8. For example, J. H. Rigg, *Modern Anglican Theology*, 3rd ed.,

London 1880, ch. IX.

9. Maurice, *Theological Essays*, p. 469.

10. Richard Whately, *Essays on Some of the Peculiarities of the Christian Religion*, Oxford 1825, Essay I.

11. A. F. Hort, *The Life and Letters of F. J. A. Hort*, Macmillan 1896, vol. I, pp. 116ff.

12. *Life of Maurice*, II, p. 15.

13. *The Works of William Paley, DD*, with a Life by Alexander Chalmers, London 1821, vol. I, p. vii.

14. Ibid., V, pp. 412ff.

15. *Life of Maurice*, II, pp. 16f.

16. Ibid., p. 20.

17. O. Pfleiderer, *The Development of Theology in Germany since Kant, and its Progress in Great Britain since 1825*, London 1890, p. 373.

18. W. C. Kneale, 'Time and Eternity in Theology', *Proceedings of the Royal Aristotelian Society*, 1960–61, pp. 87–108.

19. Maurice, *Theological Essays*, pp. 464f.

20. Kneale, op. cit. See also Nelson Pike, *God and Timelessness*, Routledge & Kegan Paul 1970, *passim*.

21. H. L. Mansel, *An Examination of the Rev. F. D. Maurice's Strictures on the Bampton Lectures of 1858*, London 1859, p. 10 note K, pp. 38, 61f., and 90.

22. D. Z. Phillips, *Death and Immortality*, Macmillan 1970, esp. ch. 3.

4. The Resurrection: a Disagreement

1. Don Cupitt, *Christ and the Hiddenness of God*, Lutterworth Press 1971, pp. 173f.

2. C. F. D. Moule, *The Phenomenon of the New Testament*, SCM Press 1967, p. 13.

5. Darwinism and English Religious Thought

1. John Hick, *The Existence of God*, Macmillan 1964, pp. 103f.

2. *More Letters of Charles Darwin*, ed. Francis Darwin and A. C. Seward, John Murray 1903, vol. I, p. 202.

3. G. J. Romanes, *Thoughts on Religion*, Longmans, Green 1895, pp. 83ff.

4. Ibid., p. 173.

5. Charles Gore, *The Incarnation of the Son of God*, John Murray 1891, pp. 31–4.

6. Gore, *Belief in Christ*, John Murray 1922, pp. 317f.

7. Gore, *Belief in God*, John Murray 1921; James A. Carpenter, *Charles Gore*, Faith Press 1960, pp. 73ff.

6. An Open Letter on Exorcism

1. *The Letters of Charles Dickens*, vol. IV, 1844–1846, ed. Kathleen Tillotson, Clarendon Press 1977, p. 248.

2. Martin Bucer (1491–1551) arrived in England in 1549, the year of

the first Edwardine Prayer Book. In 1550 he was invited to write a review and criticism of it, and one of the points he took up was the Prayer Book's retention of the baptismal exorcism. His objection was that it seemed to imply that the unbaptized are demoniacs, and this is a misunderstanding of the nature of demonic possession as it is represented in the synoptic gospels. Jesus' exorcisms were miraculous and extraordinary, and ought not to be 'routinized' in church practice.

We may perhaps see in this the beginnings of an awareness of historical and cultural change. Bucer sees that the world of the gospels is different from that of the modern church, and that exorcisms performed today cannot be the same as the exorcisms performed by Jesus.

3. Charles Harris, 'Visitation of the Sick', in *Liturgy and Worship*, ed. W. Lowther Clarke, SPCK 1932, pp. 472ff.

12. *Critical Christian Ethics*

1. From 'The Present Crisis' by James Russell Lowell.

Index of Names